READINGS ON

FYODOR DOSTOYEVSKY

OTHER TITLES IN THE GREENHAVEN PRESS LITERARY COMPANION SERIES:

AMERICAN AUTHORS

Maya Angelou
Stephen Crane
Emily Dickinson
William Faulkner
F. Scott Fitzgerald
Nathaniel Hawthorne
Ernest Hemingway
Herman Melville
Arthur Miller
Eugene O'Neill
Edgar Allan Poe
John Steinbeck
Mark Twain

BRITISH AUTHORS

Jane Austen
Joseph Conrad
Charles Dickens

WORLD AUTHORS

Homer
Sophocles

AMERICAN LITERATURE

The Great Gatsby
Of Mice and Men
The Scarlet Letter

BRITISH LITERATURE

Animal Farm
The Canterbury Tales
Lord of the Flies
Romeo and Juliet
Shakespeare: The Comedies
Shakespeare: The Sonnets
Shakespeare: The Tragedies
A Tale of Two Cities

WORLD LITERATURE

The Diary of a Young Girl

Buder Branch

THE GREENHAVEN PRESS
Literary Companion
TO WORLD AUTHORS

READINGS ON

FYODOR DOSTOYEVSKY

David Bender, *Publisher*
Bruno Leone, *Executive Editor*
Brenda Stalcup, *Managing Editor*
Bonnie Szumski, *Series Editor*
Tamara Johnson, *Book Editor*

Greenhaven Press, San Diego, CA

Every effort has been made to trace the owners of copyrighted material. The articles in this volume may have been edited for content, length, and/or reading level. The titles have been changed to enhance the editorial purpose of the Opposing Viewpoints® concept. Those interested in locating the original source will find the complete citation on the first page of each article.

Library of Congress Cataloging-in-Publication Data

Readings on Fyodor Dostoyevsky / Tamara Johnson, book editor.
        p.   cm. — (The Greenhaven Press literary companion to world authors)
    Includes bibliographical references and index.
    ISBN 1-56510-588-5 (lib. bdg. : alk. paper). —
ISBN 1-56510-587-7 (pbk. : alk. paper)
    1. Dostoyevsky, Fyodor, 1821–1881—Criticism and interpretation. I. Johnson, Tamara. II. Title: Fyodor Dostoyevsky. III. Series.
PG3328.Z6R4   1998
891.73'3—DC21   97-22685
                                                                               CIP

Cover photo: Archive Photos

Copyright ©1998 by Greenhaven Press, Inc.
PO Box 289009
San Diego, CA 92198-9009
Printed in the U.S.A.

"Without war, man becomes sclerotic from living in comfort and wealth and completely loses his capacity for generous ideas and feelings, and imperceptibly becomes brutal and lapses into barbarism.... Without suffering, happiness cannot be understood."

—Fyodor Dostoyevsky, from
The Selected Letters of Dostoyevsky

Contents

Chapter 1: Major Themes in Dostoyevsky's Works

Chapter 2: *Crime and Punishment*

Chapter 3: *The Idiot*

Chapter 4: *Notes from the Underground*

Chapter 5: *The Brothers Karamazov*

as if by accident. By observing the sometimes tragic, sometimes comic actions of the novel's characters, we are allowed to come to our own conclusion on the subject of human suffering and religion without the intrusion of the author's moral stance.

FOREWORD

*"'Tis the good reader that
makes the good book."*

Ralph Waldo Emerson

The story's bare facts are simple: The captain, an old and scarred seafarer, walks with a peg leg made of whale ivory. He relentlessly drives his crew to hunt the world's oceans for the great white whale that crippled him. After a long search, the ship encounters the whale and a fierce battle ensues. Finally the captain drives his harpoon into the whale, but the harpoon line catches the captain about the neck and drags him to his death.

A simple story, a straightforward plot—yet, since the 1851 publication of Herman Melville's *Moby-Dick*, readers and critics have found many meanings in the struggle between Captain Ahab and the whale. To some, the novel is a cautionary tale that depicts how Ahab's obsession with revenge leads to his insanity and death. Others believe that the whale represents the unknowable secrets of the universe and that Ahab is a tragic hero who dares to challenge fate by attempting to discover this knowledge. Perhaps Melville intended Ahab as a criticism of Americans' tendency to become involved in well-intentioned but irrational causes. Or did Melville model Ahab after himself, letting his fictional character express his anger at what he perceived as a cruel and distant god?

Although literary critics disagree over the meaning of *Moby-Dick*, readers do not need to choose one particular interpretation in order to gain an understanding of Melville's novel. Instead, by examining various analyses, they can gain numerous insights into the issues that lie under the surface of the basic plot. Studying the writings of literary critics can also aid readers in making their own assessments of *Moby-Dick* and other literary works and in developing analytical thinking skills.

The Greenhaven Literary Companion Series was created with these goals in mind. Designed for young adults, this unique anthology series provides an engaging and comprehensive introduction to literary analysis and criticism. The essays included in the Literary Companion Series are chosen for their accessibility to a young adult audience and are expertly edited in consideration of both the reading and comprehension levels of this audience. In addition, each essay is introduced by a concise summation that presents the contributing writer's main themes and insights. Every anthology in the Literary Companion Series contains a varied selection of critical essays that cover a wide time span and express diverse views. Wherever possible, primary sources are represented through excerpts from authors' notebooks, letters, and journals and through contemporary criticism.

Each title in the Literary Companion Series pays careful consideration to the historical context of the particular author or literary work. In-depth biographies and detailed chronologies reveal important aspects of authors' lives and emphasize the historical events and social milieu that influenced their writings. To facilitate further research, every anthology includes primary and secondary source bibliographies of articles and/or books selected for their suitability for young adults. These engaging features make the Greenhaven Literary Companion Series ideal for introducing students to literary analysis in the classroom or as a library resource for young adults researching the world's great authors and literature.

Exceptional in its focus on young adults, the Greenhaven Literary Companion Series strives to present literary criticism in a compelling and accessible format. Every title in the series is intended to spark readers' interest in leading American and world authors, to help them broaden their understanding of literature, and to encourage them to formulate their own analyses of the literary works that they read. It is the editors' hope that young adult readers will find these anthologies to be true companions in their study of literature.

INTRODUCTION

Fyodor Dostoyevsky ranks among the greatest writers in history. His novels, including *Crime and Punishment, The Brothers Karamazov,* and *The Idiot,* are classics on a scale with the works of Shakespeare and Sophocles. He was also an innovator: The philosophical ramblings of characters such as Raskolnikov and the Underground Man foreshadow the ideas of French existentialist writers such as Jean-Paul Sartre and Albert Camus. The psychological perception and analysis found in his books astounded later experts in psychology including Sigmund Freud. Dostoyevsky continues to provide inspiration to other writers and even filmmakers such as Akira Kurasawa, whose Japanese version of *The Idiot* is a classic in its own right. Around the world, the work of Dostoyevsky is as important today as it was a century ago.

In *The Greenhaven Press Literary Companion to Fyodor Dostoyevsky,* important writers and scholars from around the world wrestle with the timeless questions proposed by Dostoyevsky's novels. Their essays attempt to answer questions from a variety of perspectives, some philosophical, others psychological, ethical, or political. These varied approaches allow students to discover diverse materials from which to generate topics for research papers, group studies, and oral presentations.

The essays in this companion are selected and organized for students encountering Dostoyevsky for the first time. Collectively they demonstrate a range of possibilities for the beginning scholar. Some essays offer insight into Dostoyevsky's life; others put the novels in historical perspective. Still others select specific characters or images from the novels for in-depth analysis. The essays not only serve as models but represent the large numbers of studies available to students. Additional listings at the end of this book point students toward various publications that are recommended for further research.

The brief biography is designed to provide students with a basic understanding of Dostoyevsky's life: when and where he was born, his cultural background, political and historical influences on his writing, and the impact of personal events and tragedies on his novels. The timeline helps students visualize events in clear order and places Dostoyevsky's work in the context of the time in which he lived.

Contributors' essays are well supported with helpful features: Introductions to each essay clarify and summarize the main point so that the reader will know what to expect. Interspersed within the essays, the reader will find inserts that add authenticity, supplementary information, or illustrative anecdotes. Inserts are drawn from sources such as original letters by Dostoyevsky, writings from his private notebooks, and the commentary of other notable authors.

FYODOR DOSTOYEVSKY:
A BIOGRAPHY

Fyodor Dostoyevsky was born in Moscow, Russia, on October 30, 1821, the second son of Dr. Mikhail Andreyevich Dostoyevsky and Mariya Fyodorovna. Though Dostoyevsky could trace his ancestors to nobility, his own father and grandfather were humble priests, a vocation he had been expected to choose as well. Mikhail Dostoyevsky, however, had other ambitions and ran away from home at age fifteen. He applied for admission to the Imperial Medical-Surgical Academy in Moscow and was accepted. In 1812, during his last year at the academy, French emperor Napoléon led his troops in a disastrous invasion of Russia and Dostoyevsky was sent to care for the Russian wounded and sick. He was still a military doctor when he married Mariya. She was a merchant's daughter, pretty and smart, with a sophistication that belied her working-class background. Though the marriage was arranged by her family, as was the custom, the two fell deeply in love.

They had eight children together: Mikhail, born in 1820 was the eldest, one year older than Fyodor. Varvara, the third child, came four years later. The fourth child, Andrey, had a habit of tagging along with his older brothers and so was nicknamed "The Little Tail." Four years later, twins, Vera and Lyubov, were born, but only Vera survived. The last two children were Nikolay and Alexandra.

Dostoyevsky's mother was of a frail constitution and the strain of having so many children was hard on her. She was a cheerful woman, however, and enjoyed reading poetry and novels. She knew how to play guitar and had a pleasant singing voice. Sometimes her brother would stop by for a visit and the two would sing duets for the children.

Though respected, physicians were not well paid in nineteenth-century Russia. Even though Dr. Dostoyevsky's position was a prominent one, head of the Maryinsky Hospital for the Poor, he had to see private patients between his rounds at the hospital in order to make ends meet. The growing Dostoyevsky family shared a tiny apartment on the first floor of the hospital with six or seven servants. Though their presence made the already crowded apartment more cramped, Dr. Dostoyevsky considered the servants a necessity rather than an extravagance; at this time in Russian history only the poorest peasants were without hired help. In addition to the permanent help, tutors were hired to give the children their lessons and a wet nurse came every day to help care for the babies.

In part because of their mother's ill health, the care of the Dostoyevsky children was largely given over to the chief housekeeper, Alyona Frolovna, an imposing, comical woman. Weighing two hundred pounds, dipping snuff, and referring to herself as "the bride of Christ," Frolovna was kind and devoted to the family. She told the children stories of demons and hobgoblins and forbade them, on pain of dire consequences, to taste any food without first having a bite of bread. Alyona was prone to terrible nightmares and sometimes woke the entire family with her screams.

Although Alyona Frolovna kept the household running smoothly, it was Dr. Dostoyevsky who insisted that the family be kept on a strict schedule. Everyone woke up with the doctor at six o'clock. After they all had breakfast together, the children studied. Most of the children's time was spent indoors and any kind of rough or rambunctious play was forbidden. The children were expected to study as soon as they could read and so, from the age of four, Fyodor sat quietly with his books for much of the day. In the evenings, if the weather was good, the family took walks together, but mature behavior was expected. The children were absolutely not allowed to run ahead of the adults or to clown around. As an adult, Fyodor told a friend that this time had been "difficult and joyless" and brother Andrey would describe their childhood as monotonous. Still, there is no doubt that all the Dostoyevsky children respected their father and adored their mother.

DARAVOYE

In 1831 the family's routine was interrupted. The doctor was able to purchase the adjoining estates of Daravoye and

Cheramashna, about a hundred miles from Moscow. Though his salary was small, owning land had been his lifelong dream, and he sent his wife to oversee the farm and its serfs while he continued to work at the hospital. The older children stayed with their father during the year, but went to live with their mother during the summer months. At Daravoye, as they called the collective property, Fyodor was able to play in the woods unsupervised and associate with children his own age—although Fyodor and his brothers did not consider their playmates, the children of the serfs, to be their equals.

Daravoye was Fyodor's first significant contact with peasants. He watched them planting crops and played near them as they worked. A serf's life was difficult: peasants were bought and sold with the land on which they toiled, and Daravoye's poor soil made their work even harder. In addition, to feed themselves, the peasants had to work their own small plots after regular farming duties. The poorly fed, poorly clothed people of Daravoye left a strong impression on Fyodor. Later he based such pitiful characters as Lizaveta in *The Brothers Karamazov* on actual people he had observed at Daravoye as a boy.

Other encounters with the peasants of Daravoye left a different kind of impression on the young Fyodor. Once, while out picking mushrooms, Fyodor thought he heard someone cry "Wolf!" Terrified, he ran blindly out of the woods and into a man named Marey, who was walking behind his plow. Marey immediately saw how frightened Fyodor was and spoke to him with great gentleness. Though Fyodor had probably imagined the cry, the peasant treated the boy with respect, a courtesy Dostoyevsky never forgot.

School

When he was twelve, Fyodor and his brother Mikhail were sent away to boarding school. Until that time the brothers had taken lessons at home and Fyodor had grown used to studying in solitude. He did not join in the rough-and-tumble play of his schoolmates but preferred to sit and read, even in his free time, as he always had. He considered the other boys coarse, their crude language shocked him, and he looked forward to the weekends when he could go back to his father's apartment at the hospital.

One day, Fyodor recognized a new boy at the boarding school as a childhood playmate from the hospital. The other boys had circled the newcomer and were bullying him. Fyodor intervened, protecting the youth from the taunts of the older boys. Fyodor consoled the boy and checked on him in his classes from time to time, a kindness the boy never forgot. Mostly, however, Fyodor preferred the company of Mikhail to any of his other classmates. The two brothers became closer than they ever had been.

Dr. Dostoyevsky, with an eye to his sons' continuing education and future careers, arranged for their admission to the Academy of Engineers, a military school, at St. Petersburg. Neither Mikhail nor Fyodor was interested in becoming an engineer and neither was particularly well suited for the military. In fact, Mikhail was rejected from the academy on medical grounds. He was then accepted at a similar school about two hundred miles away, which meant the brothers would be, unexpectedly, separated.

A DIFFICULT TIME

While the brothers were away, their mother's health had declined. Already in a frail state, she contracted tuberculosis and, in 1836, became so weak she required care from relatives and friends. Her beautiful long hair was clipped when she could not longer comb it. Dr. Dostoyevsky consulted with other doctors at the hospital daily. Sadly, Mariya Fyodorovna died after nearly a year in bed. Several of the children were still very young. Their father was inconsolable. After his mother's death, Fyodor himself contracted an illness that left him with a hoarse, throaty voice for the rest of his life.

Still recovering from his mother's death and his subsequent illness, Fyodor left for St. Petersburg. On the way, he witnessed a scene that troubled him deeply. Fyodor, Mikhail, and their father had stopped to rest for a bit at an inn when a courier for the czar, a large red-faced man, pulled up in his carriage. The courier rushed into the station, drank a glass of vodka, and returned to his carriage, which was being driven by a young peasant. Immediately the courier began to beat the driver on the back of the neck with his fist. As the horses pulled away, Fyodor could see the courier continuing to beat the young man, his fist pounding up and down in rhythm with the whip and the horses' hooves. This experience is thought to have been the inspiration for the horse-beating scene in *Crime and Punishment.*

At the same time that his mother died, the great writer Aleksandr Pushkin was killed in a duel. Considered Russia's premier poet, the effect of Pushkin's death on the Russian people was profound. He was revered as Shakespeare was in England or Goethe in Germany. There was no writer considered better. To Fyodor, who loved Pushkin's writing, it was another great blow. He told his father that if he were not already wearing mourning for his mother, he might have worn it for Pushkin.

His father, on the other hand, lost all care about anything after his wife's death. He quit his job at the hospital and began drinking heavily. He sent his youngest children to live with an aunt, then retired to Daravoye, where he could be seen stumbling around and talking to his dead wife. He became cruel to the servants, beating the men and abusing the women. Dostoyevsky knew little if anything about his father's decline. He wrote his father kind letters and asked for money, which his father usually sent. Within two years after his wife's death, Dr. Dostoyevsky was murdered by his own serfs under mysterious circumstances.

ST. PETERSBURG

In 1843, Fyodor Dostoyevsky finished his engineering courses and was assigned to a government job. With the modest income from his job and money from his father's estate he should have been able to live comfortably, if not luxuriously, but he was prone to extravagances. He took an apartment that was much too big and expensive and was forced to take in roommates. He gambled and dined at fine restaurants and went to expensive concerts. For the first time in his life, Fyodor Dostoyevsky had many friends and acquaintances. He enjoyed the arts and intellectual conversation and found his job as a military draftsman "tiresome as potatoes." Over the Christmas holidays he translated the French writer Honoré de Balzac's novel *Eugénie Grandet* into Russian and was happy to receive some money for its publication. He also read voraciously, as he explained in a letter to his brother Mikhail:

> I read like a fiend, and reading has a strange effect on me. I reread some books I've read before, and it's as if new strength began to stir in me. I penetrate into everything. I understand with precision, and I myself draw from this the ability to create.

He began also to study the patients of one of his roommates, a Dr. Reisenkampf. Reisenkampf, like Dostoyevsky's father, worked with the destitute, and Dostoyevsky was fascinated by the lives they led. He spent many hours listening to the stories of these patients, whose lives were so different from his own. Dostoyevsky quit his job with the government and wrote his first novel, *Poor Folk*.

While he was revising *Poor Folk*, Dostoyevsky appealed to his brother-in-law, Pyotr Andreyevich Kerapin, a man much older than his sister Varvara, to send him his portion of the estate. Kerapin had been appointed executor of Dr. Dostoyevsky's will and was not very sympathetic to Fyodor's pleading letters and sent no money. Dostoyevsky had further financial problems when Reisenkampf, tired of Dostoyevsky's financial instability, moved out of the apartment. Dostoyevsky found another roommate, Dmitry Grigorovich, a friend from engineering school. Neither Grigorovich nor Dostoyevsky had enough money even for food and lived for two weeks at a time on bread and coffee. The diet began to affect Dostoyevsky's health, causing him to have more frequent epileptic seizures.

Dostoyevsky was a perfectionist; at one point, he decided to throw away his first novel and rewrite it entirely. Eventually, however, he was able to finish *Poor Folk* to his satisfaction, and read it aloud to Grigorovich. Grigorovich liked the work immensely and showed it to a publisher friend. The friend was also impressed and showed it to Vissarion Belinsky, a very important critic who gave the novel an impressive review. Dostoyevsky appeared an overnight success story. At twenty-five, he was accepted into the top literary circles of St. Petersburg. He immediately began working on his next novel, *The Double*, followed by *The Landlady*.

THE PETRASHEVSKY CIRCLE

One spring day, shortly after the publication of *The Double*, a man questioned Dostoyevsky on the street, "May I ask what the idea for your next tale is?" The man's name was Mikhail Petrashevsky. Petrashevsky, a translator, was interested in the ideas of intellectuals such as Dostoyevsky. Every Friday, Petrashevsky invited a select group of men to his home for a light dinner, cigars, and debate. The discussion ranged from politics to religion to art and literature. Petrashevsky had a lending library of books that had been banned by the czar as subversive. Dostoyevsky eagerly borrowed these books, and so did his brother Mikhail, who by this time had moved to St. Petersburg. The books had been banned for a variety of reasons: Some of them contradicted the Russian Orthodox Church and others called for social reform, including an end to serfdom.

One of the men in the group was a handsome and charismatic young radical named Nikolay Speshnev. Speshnev urged Dostoyevsky and the other writers to produce manuscripts on forbidden subjects such as socialism and atheism that could be circulated and smuggled out of the country. Another member of the circle suggested they put together a printing press in order to copy materials. Since the government considered the printing of unauthorized texts a serious offense, parts of the printing press were obtained from a variety of sources and put together secretly. (If the printing press was actually used by the Petrashevsky circle, as they came to be known, there is no record of it.) Some of the members of the Petrashevsky circle suspected that a spy lurked among them. This, in fact, turned out to be true. At a meeting of the group, Dostoyevsky read aloud a copy of a controversial letter that the critic Belinsky had written to the famous writer Nikolay Gogol. Gogol had recently published a didactic work in which he upheld the feudal system, going so far as to advise landowners not to let their serfs read anything but the Bible so as not to propagate unrest. Belinsky had written in reply that Russia was "a huge corporation of thieves and robbers" and that the czar's regime had nothing in common with Christianity, as Christ, Belinsky wrote, was "the first to instruct mankind in liberty, equality and fraternity." For reading such a letter, Dostoyevsky, along with Speshnev and others, was arrested, charged, and convicted of antigovernment activity, a potentially capital offense.

A MOCK EXECUTION

While Dostoyevsky was isolated in prison, the court took six weeks to decide that he and fourteen others should receive the death penalty. Their cases, however, were reviewed by the highest judicial body, the Auditoriat General, which ruled:

> Retired Lieutenant Dostoyevsky for having taken part in criminal designs, having circulated a letter by the writer Belinsky which was filled with impertinent expressions against

the Orthodox Church and the sovereign power and for having attempted, together with others, to circulate works against the government through means of a private printing press, is to be stripped of all rights owing to his station and to be exiled to penal servitude in a fortress for eight years.

Dostoyevsky was lucky: Speshnev, who it is believed was Dostoyevsky's first inspiration for Stavrogin in *The Devils*, received a life sentence. But while the czar approved of the commuted sentences, he ordered that the prisoners not be told of the Auditoriat General's decision until all the formalities of an execution had taken place.

On December 22, 1849, at seven o'clock in the morning, Dostoyevsky was given his street clothes and placed in a guarded coach. He had been arrested in spring so his clothing was unsuitable for the winter weather. He was driven for some distance until the coach stopped in front of a crowd. There he was led to a platform draped in black and lined up with other prisoners, some strangers, others people he knew. Fifteen feet in front of them a firing squad was awaiting orders. The prisoners' names and sentences were pronounced: "Dostoyevsky ... condemned to capital punishment by shooting." Neither the crowds nor the prisoners knew the execution would not take place. There was a cart, with a mat covering what appeared to be coffins. A priest offered last rites and urged the convicts to confess. The firing squad was ordered to take aim, and then, dramatically, a courier jumped out of a carriage waving their reprieve and shouting, "Long live the czar! The good czar!"

Convict and Exile

In January 1850, Dostoyevsky was sent to a labor camp in Omsk, Siberia. There, along with about 160 other convicts of all sorts, he marched in shackles doing roadwork, shoveling snow, and firing bricks. He lived in a common house infested with lice and other vermin. He was denied reading material except for the New Testament, which he did read and found comforting. Most difficult for Dostoyevsky was the lack of privacy. Never before had he been among thieves and murderers, and their forced and constant companionship was torture to him.

On the other hand, he found the other prisoners' impressive abilities to evade regulations amazing. Though money was forbidden, there was brisk business in banking, gambling, and prostitution. Alcohol was sold, as were occasional food items and other contraband. Prisoners could be flogged, sometimes to death, for any infraction but seldom were caught. Dostoyevsky's prison experiences were the inspiration for *Memoirs from the House of the Dead.*

Other political prisoners were also at Omsk. Among them were the Decembrists, a group of intellectuals who had spoken out for social reform shortly after Dostoyevsky was born. Many of their wives had followed their husbands to Siberia and had devoted their lives to making prison life less brutal for Dostoyevsky and others convicted of political crimes. In addition to the Decembrists, there were common prisoners whom Dostoyevsky found admirable. Dostoyevsky considered one young man in particular completely unaffected by the experiences of the prison camp; he was likely the earliest model for Prince Myshkin of *The Idiot.* Also helpful were the hospital staff who sometimes excused Dostoyevsky from work details even when he was not suffering from seizures. Resting in the sick bay, he was able to read Dickens's *David Copperfield* and *The Pickwick Papers* and to write some notes known as the "Siberian Notebooks."

For four years, however, Dostoyevsky was not able to write or receive letters. In 1854, Dostoyevsky was allowed to serve out the last half of his sentence as a military private. He was assigned to a battalion stationed about five hundred miles southeast of Omsk, in a little town called Semipalatinsk. Only then was he able to write to Mikhail asking for books—"my life, my food, my future." The years without them had been agony. "I consider those four years as a time in which I was buried alive in a closed coffin," he wrote Andrey. "It was unspeakable, interminable suffering because every minute weighed upon my soul like a stone." One of the first books he read was Ivan Turgenev's *A Sportsman's Sketches.*

LOVE AND FRIENDSHIP

Semipalatinsk was a town of about five thousand people, mostly poor and indifferent to literary matters. Dostoyevsky was fortunate to find a friend in a twenty-one-year-old lawyer, Alexandr Vrangel, who was the district public prosecutor. Vrangel was from St. Petersburg. He was sharp, kind, and brimming with high ideals. Dostoyevsky, a former resident of St. Petersburg, reminded him of home. The two men took to each other immediately. Vrangel introduced Dostoyevsky everywhere. When Dostoyevsky was granted permission to leave the barracks, Vrangel offered him the rental of a cottage on his property and Dostoyevsky gladly accepted. There they swam and gardened, talking and smoking cigars late into the night.

Vrangel also encouraged a friendship between Dostoyevsky and the pretty wife of a poor schoolteacher. Mariya Dmitriyevna Isayeva was in sorry circumstances. Her husband, Alexandr, was an alcoholic and could not keep a job. She, like Dostoyevsky's mother, suffered from tuberculosis and was having difficulty supporting her young son, Pasha. Vrangel lent Dostoyevsky money to give to Mariya and, when her husband was offered a job five hundred miles to the northeast, Vrangel kept Alexandr Isayeva drunk on champagne so that his friend could spend the last few hours with Mariya, with whom he had, by then, fallen deeply in love.

When Mariya left, Dostoyevsky was devastated. He could not eat or drink and compared her departure to his arrest in 1849. He was in his early thirties yet had never been in love before. Dostoyevsky and Mariya continued to write and when Dostoyevsky confided to Vrangel just how miserable he was, Vrangel arranged a rendezvous for the pair. Mariya, however, did not show. Then, suddenly, Alexandr Isayeva died. Dostoyevsky frantically borrowed more money from Vrangel to send to the widow, but he was not allowed to leave Semipalatinsk to be with her.

Dostoyevsky wanted to marry Mariya, but she was unsure. She had been married to one poor man and did not want to marry another. Dostoyevsky was only a private in the military and not allowed to publish his work. Vrangel and other influential friends began to lobby the government on his behalf. He must be allowed to publish, they argued. His rank should be increased. He himself wrote to General Deuard Todtleben, who had been a schoolmate of one of his brothers, repenting the error of his ways and admitting that his punishment had been just. He would be a loyal subject from that moment on. On November 20, 1855, Dostoyevsky was promoted to the rank of noncommissioned officer. One year later he was promoted to second lieutenant. This was enough to persuade Mariya. They were married on February 6, 1857. Six months later his first short story since his imprisonment, "The Little Hero," was published.

AT WORK AGAIN

In 1858 Dostoyevsky was released from the service and freed from Semipalatinsk, though he was denied permission to go to either Moscow or St. Petersburg. He and Mariya chose Tver, a town not far from Moscow, but were unimpressed with their new home. While there, he completed two more novels, *The Uncle's Dream* and *The Friend of the Family*, but his effort to avoid controversy with the censors showed, and neither was among his best. His brother Mikhail agreed to become his literary agent and Dostoyevsky continued to ask for permission to move to St. Petersburg. By Christmas 1859, ten years after he left for Siberia, Dostoyevsky was allowed to return to the city he loved.

In January 1860, a two-volume collection of Dostoyevsky's work was published. Then, in July, Mikhail received permission to publish a magazine, called *Vremya*, or *Time*, in part a vehicle for his talented younger brother. Dostoyevsky's next major work, *The Insulted and Injured*, was presented in installments beginning with the very first issue. When Dostoyevsky's next major work, *Memoirs from the House of the Dead*, had trouble with the censors at another magazine, *Time* published it as well. In June 1862, Dostoyevsky traveled to Germany, France, and England. Later that year he visited Switzerland and Italy. His impressions of Europe, called *Winter Notes and Summer Impressions*, were published in *Time*.

Meanwhile, both he and Mariya were becoming increasingly ill—his epileptic seizures and Mariya's tuberculosis worsened. Unable to withstand the harsh winters in St. Petersburg, Mariya moved back to Tver, where the weather was milder, and Dostoyevsky returned to Europe on the advice of his doctors, who recommended expert medical consultation in Berlin and Paris. While in Europe, Dostoyevsky renewed a relationship with a young female writer who had been a onetime contributor to *Time*, Apollinariya Suslova.

This was a destructive period in Dostoyevsky's life. Dostoyevsky was in constant need of money, compulsively losing at the roulette wheel whatever relatives sent him. These months would be the inspiration for his short novel *The Gambler*. His relationship with Apollinariya was destructive and frustrating as well. He alternated between the roles of father figure, listening to her accounts of her romances with other men, and jealous lover, becoming furious with her.

Apollinariya was jealous, too, angry with Dostoyevsky for his loyalty to Mariya, whom he had no intention of divorcing. At home, things were no better; *Time* was being shut down by the censors and Mariya was growing sicker all the time.

In 1864, Mikhail received permission to start a new magazine, the *Epoch,* to which Dostoyevsky contributed his most bitter work up to that point. *Notes from the Underground* was the story of a lonely and hypersensitive outsider who is obsessed with inflicting humiliation on himself and other people. The target of Dostoyevsky's cruel wit was an earnest young socialist, Nikolay Chernyshevsky, who had been sentenced to Siberia for his novel *What Is to Be Done?,* but the self-loathing of the author was evident in the novel's Underground Man as well. Not long after *Notes from the Underground,* Dostoyevsky's wife succumbed to tuberculosis. Shortly after Mariya's death, Mikhail died from an infection of the spleen. Dostoyevsky tried to keep the last magazine alive, but without his brother's management skills, the *Epoch* folded.

FINANCIAL STRUGGLES CONTINUE

Devastated by the recent tragedies, Dostoyevsky was under new financial pressures. The magazine had accumulated considerable debt, which he was obliged to pay off. Also, Mikhail had left a wife and family whom Dostoyevsky felt an additional obligation to support. He was, in addition, desperately lonely. In April 1865, he proposed to a young writer, Anna Korvin-Krukovskaya, but she turned him down. He unsuccessfully sought an advance on a novel called *The Drunkards,* later to become *Crime and Punishment.* He attempted to borrow money from friends and even a few people he was not so friendly with. Finally, a book dealer named F.T. Stellovsky bought the right to publish all his works in three volumes. The terms were that Dostoyevsky must complete a new novel by November 1866. If Dostoyevsky failed to deliver the novel by the first of December, he would forfeit all rights to his works. He gave some of the 3,000-ruble advance to Mikhail's widow and most of the rest to his creditors. Then, with 178 rubles in his pocket, he went back to Germany to see Apollinariya Suslovna.

The trip was not a successful one. In Wiesbaden he gambled away the little money he had. Suslovna, too, had no money and left for Paris shortly after Dostoyevsky's arrival.

Dostoyevsky wrote to her:

> You had just left, and on the following day, early in the morning, the people here at the hotel informed me that they'd been instructed not to give me dinner, tea, or coffee. I went to clear up the misunderstanding and the fat German proprietor informed me that I don't "deserve" any dinner and that he would send me only tea. And so since yesterday I've not eaten dinner, and am living only on tea. . . . The German knows no greater crime than to be without money and not to pay one's bills promptly.

Dostoyevsky was miserable. He spent day and night in the cramped hotel room working on *Crime and Punishment,* at times without even a candle. He asked everyone he could think of for money, including Turgenev, who was living in Germany, and whose book *A Sportsman's Sketches* had been one of the first books he had read after his imprisonment. Finally, his old friend Vrangel received two of his letters and invited Dostoyevsky to Copenhagen, where he was then stationed. Dostoyevsky stayed with Vrangel for ten days before returning to Russia, where he lived, happily for a time, with his sister Vera and her nine children.

Back in St. Petersburg, Dostoyevsky decided *Crime and Punishment* was unsatisfactory and burned the entire novel. He had, however, found a publisher for the novel, and agreed to rewrite it, in installments, for the *Russian Messenger.* He was sick and had sold all his possessions, including most of his clothes, and was now under pressure to meet deadlines, intensified when the editors found one of his installments too controversial and forced Dostoyevsky to rewrite it. Fortunately, the magazine was often issued late, and he was able to meet his deadlines.

Obsessed with completing *Crime and Punishment,* Dostoyevsky had nearly put his other deadline, the one with the bookdealer Stellovsky, out of his mind. In October he realized he had a little over a month in which to complete an entire novel. Desperate, he turned to an acquaintance who was the director of a secretarial school to help with the typing. The acquaintance sent Dostoyevsky his best pupil, twenty-year-old Anna Grigoryevna Snitkina, who had read Dostoyevsky's works and was excited to have the job although she found the famous author strange and intimidating. The novel, which would later be called *The Gambler,* was full of vice and sexual intrigue. Dostoyevsky confided in Anna the details of his time with Apollinariya and other women.

While another young woman might have been shocked at the coarse subject matter and Dostoyevsky's gruff manner, Anna Grigoryevna remained calm and professional. They finished the novel on October 30, Dostoyevsky's forty-fifth birthday. On February 15, 1867, the two were married.

LIFE WITH ANNA

To escape continuing debts, Dostoyevsky moved once more to Europe, this time taking his new bride with him. Anna was under no illusions about her husband's eccentricities and ill health. He attempted to keep no secrets, including his compulsive gambling, from her. Three months after they arrived in Europe, Dostoyevsky left Anna in Dresden while he went to Hamburg to play the roulette tables. Soon, he had lost all the money they had taken with them. In subsequent months they were forced to pawn her jewelry, including her wedding ring, both of their coats, and a lace shawl. He was again borrowing money from anyone who would lend it to them. Such difficulties did not much affect Dostoyevsky's writing, however, and it was during this period that *The Idiot* was written.

The Dostoyevskys then moved to Switzerland, where in February 1868 their daughter was born. The couple was ecstatic, but three months later the infant died of pneumonia. Wishing to leave painful reminders behind, Fyodor and Anna then moved to Italy, impressed by its cultural and architectural riches. Anna, however, was pregnant again, and as neither of them spoke Italian, they decided to move back to Germany, where at least they could communicate with doctors should an emergency arise. In May 1869, another daughter, Lyubov, was born and Anna's mother came to live with them awhile. For a time the gambling subsided and Dostoyevsky, though homesick, was as content as he had ever been.

The creation of *The Devils*, however, was agonizing work. Dostoyevsky spent as much time writing it as he had writing both *The Idiot* and *Crime and Punishment.* He still had not completed it when the little family returned to St. Petersburg in 1871. He would never be entirely happy with the novel. Eight days after their return to St. Petersburg, Anna gave birth to a son, Fyodor.

Though they immediately faced unpaid bills, Anna proved to be a competent businesswoman. She was able to placate creditors, rent an apartment in her name and obtain furniture on an installment plan so that it legally belonged to the shop until fully paid for and therefore could not be seized to satisfy a debt. She also decided to publish her husband's work herself and to sell it out of the house, a venture that was surprisingly successful. Nevertheless, the family remained in debt until the last year of Dostoyevsky's life.

They had another son, Alyosha, whom Dostoyevsky doted on. When Dostoyevsky developed emphysema in addition to his epilepsy and had to leave for extended periods for treatment, he wrote long letters full of love and worry for his wife and children. He continued to work despite his ill health, and even accepted an editorship at the magazine *Citizen.* The family took summer trips together. On one of these expeditions, Dostoyevsky left the family for a short period to visit his sister Vera, who was then living at the old summer home at Daravoye.

Anna sold *The Diary of a Writer,* Dostoyevsky's longest single work, out of their home in installments. Anna took on the exhausting jobs of transcribing, bookkeeping, distributing, and negotiating all deals with the printers and booksellers, freeing the writer to do only what he did best. No period of complacency was to last long, however; in 1878, Dostoyevsky was to suffer another tragedy. His beloved son Alyosha died at age three due to epilepsy. Blaming himself, through his hereditary illness, for the boy's death, the devastated Dostoyevsky left town for a time to seek the advice of a Russian Orthodox monk he knew of.

THE BROTHERS KARAMAZOV

Drawing on his personal tragedies, *The Brothers Karamazov* was the last of Dostoyevsky's great novels. It is the story of a father's murder, a priest's wisdom, and a good son named Alyosha. No other work of Dostoyevsky's was greeted with such enthusiasm. Leo Tolstoy, himself one of the greatest Russian writers of all time, declared the book the best of the century, ranking with Pushkin, Dostoyevsky's early hero. At the unveiling of a statue of Pushkin, Dostoyevsky and Turgenev were among those asked to make speeches. In a letter to Anna, Dostoyevsky described the reception that awaited his address:

> The hall was packed. . . . When I appeared thunderous clapping burst out, and for a long, long time they would not let me

speak. I kept bowing and making signs . . . but it was no use. There was ecstasy and enthusiasm, all due to the Karama- zovs. . . . I spoke loudly and fervently. (What a colossal tri- umph of our ideas over a quarter of a century of errors!) But at the end when I held for the *world-wide unity* of people, the hall seemed to be having hysterics. When I'd finished—I can't convey to you the howl, the shriek of ecstasy. Strangers among the audience were crying, sobbing, embracing *and swearing to be better men, not to hate each other in future, but to love.* The meeting broke up and everyone rushed toward me on the platform.

He had become well known in his native land. Though he planned other works, Dostoyevsky's ill health got the best of him and he would never finish another novel. When he died on January 28, 1881, thirty thousand people came to see his coffin carried to the Tikhvinsky cemetery.

CHAPTER 1

Major Themes in Dostoyevsky's Works

READINGS ON
FYODOR DOSTOYEVSKY

Dostoyevsky's Interest in the Criminal Mind

Erik Krag

The Memoirs from the House of the Dead marks a change of direction for Dostoyevsky. It is in this largely autobiographical novel based on the author's experience living among hardened prisoners in a Siberian labor camp, that we are first introduced to the workings of the truly criminal mind. In this excerpt, translated from the Norwegian, Oslo professor Erik Krag offers evidence that Dostoyevsky's fascination with the life of the great sinner is the result of astute observation rather than (as Freud and others have suggested) a personal propensity for crime. By using Dostoyevsky's personal letters as well as alternate versions of the memoirs, Krag shows how Dostoyevsky's careful studies of his fellow convicts formed not only the foundation for this work of "prison literature," but the impetus for subsequent novels as well.

The literal title, 'Memoirs from a Dead House,' does not denote a house where there have been deaths, where death has ravaged, but rather a house where life stands still or has stagnated.

The work first appeared in full in 1861 in *Time (Vremia)*, a literary journal edited jointly by Dostoevsky and his brother Mikhail, and came out in book form in 1862. It covers the period 1850-1854, during which Dostoevsky was in prison near Omsk in Siberia.

A HELLISH ORDEAL

The book appeared at a promising and important time in Russian history. A period of liberalization had arrived; the early 1860's was the 'time of the great reforms.' In February

From Erik Krag, *Dostoevsky: The Literary Artist*, translated by Sven Larr (Oslo: Universitetsforlaget and New York: Humanities Press, 1976). Copyright ©1976 by The Norwegian Research Council for Science and the Humanities. Reprinted by permission of the Scandinavian University Press, Oslo.

1861 serfdom was abolished, to be followed by significant reforms of the judicial system. [As one critic,] A.P. Milyukov, rightly comments:

> This work [*Memoirs...*] appeared under quite favorable cir-
> cumstances. Within the censorship there prevailed at that
> time a spirit of tolerance, and works of literature were pub-
> lished which only a short time ago would never have seen the
> light of day. Though the novelty of the book, devoted wholly
> to the life of convicts, the dark canvas of its numerous stories
> about the most awful villains, and, finally, the fact that the
> author himself was a recently returned political criminal, did
> slightly trouble the censor, Dostoevsky did not compromise
> in the least with the truth, and the *Memoirs from the House of
> the Dead* made a shattering impact. The author, as it were,
> was seen as a new Dante who had descended into hell, a hell
> all the more terrible in that it did not exist in the author's fan-
> tasy but in reality.

It could be added that Dostoevsky's Inferno 'in reality' was even worse than what we come to know in the *Memoirs*. To be sure, what is related here is personally experienced and authentic. But the relatively long period of time that elapsed between the experience and its reconstruction has taken the edge off much of it. And partly the task itself, of giving an artistic representation of personal experience, caused the author to tone down and gloss over a few things. In a letter to his brother Mikhail written in February 1854, immedi-ately after his release, Dostoevsky gives largely the same ac-count of his life in prison as in the *Memoirs*, but the tone is quite different. About his fellow convicts he writes:

> They are coarse, exasperated, and embittered people. Their
> hatred of the nobility knows no bounds, and therefore they
> met us gentlefolk with hostility and gloated over our misfor-
> tune. They would have devoured us if they had been allowed
> to. Incidentally, you may judge for yourself how well pro-
> tected we were, having to live, eat, drink, and sleep together
> with those people year after year, suffering countless indig-
> nities of all sorts, so many, indeed, that time would not have
> sufficed for all our complaints.... One hundred and fifty en-
> emies never grew tired of persecuting us; it was a pleasure to
> them, an amusement, something to occupy them.... They
> had no clear idea of our crime. We ourselves maintained si-
> lence on the matter, and therefore we did not understand one
> another; consequently, we had to endure all the vengeance
> and persecution [intended for] ... the nobility.

Daily life in the prison is also described in more glaring col-ors than in the *Memoirs:*

> We were lumped together all of us in a barracks. . . . All the
> floors were completely rotten. The dirt on the floor was more
> than an inch thick, so you could slip and fall. . . . You'd make
> a fire with six logs of wood but there would be no heat, . . .
> only unbearable smoke; all winter it was like that. The pris-
> oners washed their underclothes right there in the barracks,
> splashing water all over the little room.

He also mentions the *ushat*, the latrine bucket which was
put out for the night, spreading an insufferable stench, and
a host of 'fleas, lice, and roaches, bucketfuls of them.'

Apart from artistic considerations, for reasons of censorship alone Dostoevsky's naturalism in depicting the details
of his prison experience tends to be fairly subdued.

This may be just as well. Nowadays, at any rate, we would
not have been greatly impressed by a naturalistic account,
though in Dostoevsky's time it may have been different.
When, toward the end of the century, the American journal-
ist George Kennan gave a description of the contemporary
Siberian prisons that confirms some of the worst features
mentioned in Dostoevsky's letter, his book created a sensation all over the world, so unheard-of and ghastly did the
whole picture appear. Our age, however, has become con-
siderably more callous in regard to such matters. Today a
great many people have had experiences matching, even
surpassing the massive horror that Dostoevsky went through
in Siberia, and there exists a considerable literature about
time spent in jails and work camps.

PRISON EXPERIENCE OFFERS INSIGHT

What has made this book, all the same, into something
unique in world literature? Partly, of course, it is the author's
genius, his ability to identify himself with the inner life of the
people he was brought in contact with. Partly also it springs
from something peculiar in his situation, evident from the
above quotation. His situation was essentially different from
that of prisoners in a concentration camp in time of war. The
latter entered into a large community where all previous di-
visions vanished. Dostoevsky, on the other hand, was between the devil and the deep blue sea. He was sentenced as
a criminal by the authorities, but was viewed as an enemy by
his fellow prisoners; he was looked down upon and met with
mistrust and resentment. This produced a fatiguing psychological tension. On the one hand there was the torture of
never being alone that he conveys so convincingly; on the

other he experienced a continuous sense of spiritual loneliness in the midst of the crowd, as if he were a stranger or an emigrant, an outcast among outcasts. Both socially and mentally there was a great gulf. However, the barrier between Dostoevsky and the other inmates was not of his making. . . . Actually, he found that some of these people were both exceptionally intelligent and possessed uncommon strength of character. He says himself that many of the nation's strongest and most gifted people were landed in Siberian jail. Some were riddles to him, such as the fearless, arrogant, iron-willed Orlov. Others had become insensitive—animals in human form. There were also those who had come to a life of crime almost through weakness, by chance, 'bad breaks.' With a few quick strokes Dostoevsky portrays this wide assortment of different types and makes searching studies of their inner lives.

A CHANGE IN FOCUS

There can be no doubt that Dostoevsky's profound knowledge of sin and crime, along with his interest in criminals and in 'the great sinner,' stems from his prison experience in Siberia. Until then he had described petty government clerks and young dreamers. There are no real criminals in his works from the period before Siberia. Murin was a robber chief in the style of the folk ballad and the fairy tale rather than a plain criminal. As a young author Dostoevsky had a preference for the idyll and for the 'sentimental.' Only after Siberia does he acquire the ability to probe, as Shakespeare did, the minds of perpetrators of violence. He has been taken to task for this, among others by Sigmund Freud, in whose eyes it is an indication of criminal propensities in the author himself. Is it fair of Freud to equate the author and his characters? . . .

Dostoevsky's understanding of the criminal was surely not inborn, but was acquired at a high price. It cost him four years of enforced consorting with brigands and murderers in Siberia.

His objectivity in *Memoirs from the House of the Dead* is unquestionable: he is willing to let his own person recede into the background and to let things speak for themselves. Admittedly, it is easy to see through the fiction of the condemned criminal, a wife-killer by the name of Aleksander Petrovich Goryanchikov, who is said to be the author of the *Memoirs*. After the fashion of many other authors, from

Pushkin to Kierkegaard, Dostoevsky acts only as 'editor.' In his case it may have been intended as a lever to place him in a somewhat freer position in regard to the censor. But, of course, no one believes in Goryanchikov, and it is Dostoevsky's own voice that we hear throughout. Nevertheless, the account is objective. In contrast to the tone of Dostoevsky the novelist, this is a calm and dispassionate voice.

THE BOOK'S CONTENTS DETAILED

The book consists of two parts. In Part I the composition follows chronologically. The first four chapters deal with the first day in the prison. The author begins by broadly sketching a large general picture: the fortress, the jail, the rampart, the barracks and the prison yard surrounded by a stockade, on the stakes of which Dostoevsky used to count the days. Further, he describes the activities in the various workshops and on the banks of the Irtysh, the prisoners, their appearance, occupations, and behavior, singling out a few conspicuous faces among the branded men. The master of dialog runs true to form: from the very moment the prisoners turn out in the morning he notes many a characteristic saying and numerous quirks of speech. In the course of the day a series of dramatic episodes take place, mainly involving convicts who go on the spree. In the evening, when they have settled on their bunks, a prisoner will tell his story to his bunkmate.

In the following chapters the narrative is broadened to take in the first month in the prison. Subjects that initially were merely outlined are now amplified, and new figures are introduced.

In the last chapters of Part I, the account is rounded off by a broad description of the entire first year. The course of the year is marked by certain high points, vividly impressive happenings like the sauna bath, the Christmas celebrations, amateur entertainments showing the deep love of art, especially theater, among ordinary Russians, and finally the great Easter festival. This brings the account of the prisoner's first year to an end; of his impressions and experiences during the remaining months of the year we are given only a few glimpses.

Part II embraces the next three years, though now there is hardly a trace of chronological order. A stay in the infirmary provides an opportunity to describe the many gruesome methods of punishment, such as running the gauntlet, caning, and knouting. ('The great reforms' entailed, among other things, abolition of these punishments; Dostoevsky expressly mentions this: 'Now, I have heard, all this has changed'.) Then comes the story 'Akulka's Husband,' a cruel but no doubt authentic tale from the lower depths. Further, there is a description of the prisoners' work during the summer months. Of considerable interest are their relations with animals (horses, etc., as shown in the chapter 'Prison Animals'). Especially moving is the story of the wounded eagle, which is kept in a cage by the convicts but at the end is set free. The story acquires symbolic significance, the eagle becoming an image of man deprived of his freedom.

REAL STORIES FROM PRISON LIFE

Finally comes what could be called the sociology of prison life. We are told how the prisoners embark upon the very risky business of voicing their grievances, an undertaking from which the narrator, a member of the upper classes, is firmly excluded. This incident leads naturally to an account of the gentlemen convicts, which is followed by a chapter about an abortive escape. The second part concludes with the narrator's release, related in a kind of epilog.

The pictures of daily life in the prison stand out by their grim power, an effect that is partly due to the deliberate conciseness and matter-of-factness of the style and the calm, almost dry tone. A climax is reached with 'The Sauna Bath.' This 'interior' derives, as it were, from hell itself: an overheated room filled with steam and stacked from floor to ceiling with naked bodies. Some lie in the mud, others stand upright splashing themselves with water from their pails, while on the shelves scores of men are frantically lashing one another with birch twigs. Passing bathers catch their chains against the heads of those sitting down or get entangled in the chains of others; they slip and fall in the muck or drag a fellow convict along with them. In the confused mass of shaven heads and steaming bodies, the prisoners' flayed backs glow with a sinister radiance as the hideous scars left by flogging momentarily take on the appearance of fresh wounds. At intervals, the armed guard outside sticks his nose through the peephole. This description was praised by Turgenev, Dostoevsky's literary opponent, as veritably 'Dantesque.' E.M. de Vogüé, author of *Le roman russe,* who otherwise shows little appreciation of Dostoevsky, also compares it with scenes from Dante's *Inferno*.

As for the convicts, one has the impression that, individually, these criminal offenders were by and large good-natured people. They are characterized by their speech, an assortment of local dialects from every corner of Russia mixed with thieves' slang, argot. Dostoevsky made careful studies of their language; a notebook that he managed to preserve throughout his stay contains several thousand adages and turns of phrase which he had immediately taken down, along with characteristic exchanges and a few snatches of song. He made generous use of this notebook material, which was later published by his widow, Anna Grigorievna; the *Memoirs* richly display the common people's passion for verbal duels, quick-witted retorts, and clever abuse. Even the most violent invective rarely leads to a fight. Apart from venting their pent-up emotions through this virtuoso abuse, the convicts also seem to derive a sort of esthetic pleasure from it.

But if many of the criminals appeared relatively good-natured, Dostoevsky also encountered truly demonic figures, people who had become hardened to evil; they are frightening and captivating at the same time. These criminals did not show the faintest trace of repentance. The author says that 'it should surely have been possible in so many years to perceive something in those hearts, to catch at least some hint, however fugitive, which revealed inward anguish or suffering. But there was nothing of the sort, definitely not'. Their lack of moral feeling could not be explained away by 'impaired mental faculties,' or by the notion that they were undeveloped. On the contrary, it was just those who were most conspicuously lacking in remorse who were the most gifted, the best educated, the strongest among the prisoners. The question of conscience is more complex than the moralists tend to believe. Dostoevsky endeavors to explore the abysses in the life of the psyche. . . .

At the end of the introduction there is the following comment about the manuscript of the fictitious author: 'In places . . . [this account] was interrupted by another narrative, some strange and terrible reminiscences that were jotted down roughly and spasmodically, as though under compulsion'. Did the author originally intend to write this gruesome story of a drama of jealousy ending with the wife's murder and perhaps insert it into the narrative of his stay in jail, constantly interweaving one with the other? Was the sober, scrupulous account of his prison experiences to be interrupted by the nightmarish reminiscences he was 'almost convinced' were written 'in madness'? This would have been a very modern form of composition. If he did have this in mind, the author dropped the idea, a fate shared both earlier and later by several others, whether they pertained to intended continuations, 'a quite different story' or 'an entirely different novel,' which dawned upon him in the process of writing.

However one decides the question of genre, the *Memoirs from the House of the Dead* is clearly a great work of 'prison literature.' It is in the same class as Silvio Pellico's *My Prisons* and Leonora Christina's *Memory of Woe,* different as these works may be from each other. If Dostoevsky had written nothing else, this work alone would have sufficed to immortalize his name.

A Sensitive Undertaking

Though censorship was relatively liberal at the time, it was nevertheless a sensitive undertaking for a recently returned political prisoner to describe his stay in prison. To paint it in too dark colors would never do, of course; but even if one emphasized certain bright spots there could be difficulties. People should not get the impression that it was pleasant to be in prison, since this might have a demoralizing effect on the readers.

The censorship committee was not satisfied with the description of certain liberties taken by the convicts at Omsk: for example, they had illegally procured white bread, liquor, and tobacco for themselves. Dostoevsky then sent in a two-page 'supplement,' in which he further amplifies what had already been so strongly emphasized in the book, namely, that there exists no greater torment for a human being than to be deprived of his freedom.

The central portion of this supplement reads:

> What is bread? People eat bread to live, but it is not life.... Try to build a palace. Furnish it with marble, pictures, gold, birds of paradise, hanging gardens, all you desire...and then enter it. Perhaps you would wish never to leave it. Perhaps really you would never leave it. You have everything: 'the best is good enough.' But then a little thing happens. They enclose your palace with a fence and tell you: 'All is yours, please enjoy yourself—except, don't take a step beyond this point.' And rest assured, in that very moment you take it

into your head to abandon your paradise and step across the fence. And what is more, all the luxury, all the comfort, merely serves to increase your suffering. Indeed, you may feel pained precisely because of this luxury.

There is no reason to regret that this addition was not included; in *The Memoirs* . . . it was superfluous. On the other hand, it points to a story written a few years later, namely *Notes from Underground.*

Dostoyevsky's Novels Reveal the Author's Criminal Inclinations

Sigmund Freud

Austrian-born neurologist Sigmund Freud developed the practice of psychoanalysis in the late nineteenth century. It was Freud's belief that the symbols and images found in a person's dreams could be analyzed and this analysis would help guide him or her to problems in everyday life. Though many of Freud's ideas were later called into question, books such as *The Interpretation of Dreams* and *Civilization and Its Discontents* are still considered staples of college reading. To illustrate his concepts of the superego, or the moral aspect of personality, and the ego, the part of our personality that we use to represent ourselves to the world, Freud often used examples taken from literature. In the following passage, he compares *The Brothers Karamazov* to two other stories of parricide, or the murder of a father: Shakespeare's *Hamlet* and Sophocles' *Oedipus Rex*—from which comes Freud's famous term "Oedipus complex."

Four facets may be distinguished in the rich personality of Dostoevsky: the creative artist, the neurotic, the moralist and the sinner. How is one to find one's way in this bewildering complexity?

The creative artist is the least doubtful: Dostoevsky's place is not far behind Shakespeare. *The Brothers Karamazov is* the most magnificent novel ever written; the episode of the Grand Inquisitor, one of the peaks in the literature of the world, can hardly be valued too highly. Before the problem of the creative artist analysis must, alas, lay down its arms.

The moralist in Dostoevsky is the most readily assailable. If we seek to rank him high as a moralist on the plea that

Excerpted from "Dostoevsky and Parricide," in *The Collected Papers*, vol. 5, by Sigmund Freud, edited by James Strachey. Published by Basic Books, Inc., by arrangement with The Hogarth Press, Ltd., and the Institute of Psycho-Analysis, London. Reprinted by permission of BasicBooks, a division of HarperCollins Publishers, Inc., and The Hogarth Press.

only a man who has gone through the depths of sin can reach the highest summit of morality, we are neglecting a doubt that arises. A moral man is one who reacts to temptation as soon as he feels it in his heart, without yielding to it.... He has not achieved the essence of morality, renunciation, for the moral conduct of life is a practical human interest.... Dostoevsky threw away the chance of becoming a teacher and liberator of humanity and made himself one with their [jailors]. The future of human civilization will have little to thank him for....

To consider Dostoevsky as a sinner or a criminal rouses violent opposition, which need not be based upon a philistine assessment of crime. The real motive for this opposition soon becomes apparent. Two traits are essential in a criminal: boundless egoism and a strong destructive impulse. Common to both of these, and a necessary condition for their expression, is absence of love, lack of an emotional appreciation of (human) objects.... [It] must be asked why there is any temptation to reckon Dostoevsky among the criminals. The answer is that it comes from his choice of material, which singles out from all others violent, murderous and egoistic characters, thus pointing to the existence of similar tendencies in his own soul, and also from certain facts in his life, like his passion for gambling and his possible admission of a sexual assault upon a young girl. The contradiction is resolved by the realization that Dostoevsky's very strong destructive instinct, which might easily have made him a criminal, was in his actual life directed mainly against his own person (inward instead of outward) and thus found expression as masochism and a sense of guilt. Nevertheless, his personality retained sadistic traits in plenty, which show themselves in his irritability, his love of tormenting and his intolerance even towards people he loved, and which appear also in the way in which, as an author, he treats his readers. Thus in little things he was a sadist towards others, and in bigger things a sadist towards himself, in fact a masochist, that is to say the mildest, kindliest, most helpful person possible.

A Diagnosis

We have selected three factors from Dostoevsky's complex personality, one quantitative and two qualitative: the extraordinary intensity of his emotional life, his perverse instinctual predisposition, which inevitably marked him out to be a sadomasochist or a criminal, and his unanalysable artistic endowment. . . . But the position is obscured by the simultaneous presence of neurosis, which, as we have said, was not in the circumstances inevitable, but which comes into being the more readily, the richer the complication which has to be mastered by the ego. For neurosis is after all only a sign that the ego has not succeeded in making a synthesis, that in attempting to do so it has forfeited its unity. . . .

[The] formula for Dostoevsky is as follows: a person of specially strong bisexual predisposition, who can defend himself with special intensity against dependence on a specially severe father. This characteristic of bisexuality comes as an addition to the components of his nature that we have already recognized. His early symptom of death-like seizures can thus be understood as a father-identification on the part of his ego, permitted by his super-ego as a punishment. 'You wanted to kill your father in order to be your father yourself. Now you *are* your father, but a dead father'—the regular mechanism of hysterical symptoms. And further: 'Now your father is killing *you.*' For the ego the death symptom is a satisfaction in phantasy of the masculine wish and at the same time a masochistic satisfaction; for the super-ego it is a punishment satisfaction, that is, a sadistic satisfaction. Both of them, the ego and the super-ego, carry on the role of father.

To sum up, the relation between the subject and his father-object, while retaining its content, has been transformed into a relation between the ego and the super-ego— a new setting on a fresh stage. . . .

It can scarcely be owing to chance that three of the masterpieces of the literature of all time—the *Oedipus Rex* of Sophocles, Shakespeare's *Hamlet,* and Dostoevsky's *The Brothers Karamazov*—should all deal with the same subject, parricide. In all three, moreover, the motive for the deed, sexual rivalry for a woman, is laid bare. . . .

It is a matter of indifference who actually committed the crime [in *The Brothers Karamazov*], psychology is only concerned to know who desired it emotionally and who welcomed it when it was done. And for that reason all of the brothers, except the contrasted figure of Alyosha, are equally guilty, the impulsive sensualist, the sceptical cynic and the epileptic criminal. . . . Dostoevsky's sympathy for the criminal is, in fact, boundless; it goes far beyond the pity which the unhappy wretch might claim, and reminds us of the 'holy awe' with which epileptics and lunatics were regarded in the past. A criminal is to him almost a Redeemer, who has taken on himself the guilt which must else have been borne by others. There is no longer any need for one to murder, since *he* has already murdered; and one must be grateful to him, for, except for him, one would have been obliged oneself to murder. . . . This may perhaps be quite generally the mechanism of kindly sympathy with other people, a mechanism which one can discern with especial ease in the extreme case of the guilt-ridden novelist. There is no doubt that this sympathy by identification was a decisive factor in determining Dostoevsky's choice of material. He dealt first with the common criminal (whose motives are egotistical) and the political and religious criminal; and not until the end of his life did he come back to the primal criminal, the parricide, and use him, in a work of art, for making his confession.

Dostoyevsky Wrote Humane Tragedies

Oscar Wilde

Oscar Wilde was an Irish-born poet, playwright, and novelist. Among his most famous works are *The Picture of Dorian Gray* and *The Importance of Being Earnest*. In this excerpt, from *The Artist as Critic: The Critical Writings of Oscar Wilde*, Dostoyevsky's characters are compared to those that appear in Greek tragedies and in Bible stories.

Doistoieffski differs widely from ... his rivals. ... [H]e has qualities that are distinctively and absolutely his own, such as a fierce intensity of passion and concentration of impulse, a power of dealing with the deepest mysteries of psychology and the most hidden springs of life, and a realism that is pitiless in its fidelity, and terrible because it is true. Some time ago we had occasion to draw attention to his marvellous novel *Crime and Punishment,* where in the haunt of impurity and vice a harlot and an assassin meet together to read the story of Lazarus and Dives, and the outcast girl leads the sinner to make atonement for his sin; nor is the book entitled *Injury and Insult* at all inferior to that great masterpiece. Mean and ordinary though the surroundings of the story may seem, the heroine Natasha is like one of the noble victims of Greek tragedy, she is Antigone with the passions of Phaedra, and it is impossible to approach her without a feeling of awe. ... Aleosha, the beautiful young lad whom Natasha follows to her doom, is a second Tito Melema, and has all Tito's charm, and grace, and fascination. Yet he is different. He would never have denied Baldassare in the square at Florence, nor lied to Romola about Tessa. He has a magnificent, momentary sincerity; a boyish unconsciousness of all that life signifies; an ardent enthusiasm for all that life cannot give. There is nothing calculating about him. He

Excerpted from Oscar Wilde, "Dostoevsky's 'The Insulted and Injured'" (1887), in *The Artist as Critic: Critical Writings of Oscar Wilde*, edited by Richard Ellman (London: W.H. Allen, 1970).

never thinks evil, he only does it. From a psychological point of view he is one of the most interesting characters of modern fiction, as from an artistic standpoint he is one of the most attractive. As we grow to know him, he stirs strange questions for us, and makes us feel that it is not the wicked only who do wrong, nor the bad alone who work evil. And by what a subtle objective method does Doistoieffski show us his characters! He never tickets them with a list, nor labels them with a description. We grow to know them very gradually, as we know people whom we meet in society, at first by little tricks of manner, personal appearance, fancies in dress and the like; and afterwards by their deeds and words; and even then they constantly elude us, for though Doistoieffski may lay bare for us the secrets of their nature, yet he never explains his personages away, they are always surprising us by something that they say or do, and keep to the end the eternal mystery of life. Irrespective of its value as a work of art, this novel possesses a deep autobiographical interest also, as the character of Vania, the poor student who loves Natasha through all her sin and shame is Doistoieffski's study of himself. . . . [Almost] before he had arrived at manhood Doistoieffski knew life in its most real forms; poverty and suffering, pain and misery, prison, exile, and love were soon familiar to him, and by the lips of Vania he has told his own story. This note of personal feeling, this harsh reality of actual experience, undoubtedly gives the book something of its strange fervour and terrible passion, yet it has not made it egotistic; we see things from every point of view, and we feel, not that Fiction has been trammelled by fact, but that fact itself has become ideal and imaginative. Pitiless too though Doistoieffski is in his method, as an artist, yet as a man he is full of human pity for all, for those who do evil as well as for those who suffer it, for the selfish no less than for those whose lives are wrecked for others, and whose sacrifice is in vain. Since "Adam Bede," and *Le Père Goriot,* no more powerful novel has been written than [*Injury and Insult*].

The Solitary and the Profound in Dostoyevsky's Novels

André Gide

Nobel Prize–winning poet, novelist, and essayist André Gide did much to popularize Dostoyevsky in France. Gide's translations and analyses of Dostoyevsky's work were some of the first in Europe and are still widely read. In the following excerpt, from the introduction to his book *Dostoevsky*, Gide responds to some of Dostoyevsky's earliest critics who found the Russian's novels unrealistic and grim. Using examples from the major works, as well as a quote from Dostoyevsky himself, Gide shows how Dostoyevsky's stories lock well-developed and complex characters in a private struggle with some of humanity's most pressing concerns.

Dostoevsky's admirers were recently rare enough, but as invariably happens when the earliest enthusiasts are recruited from the élite, their number goes on increasing steadily. First of all, I should like to inquire how it is that certain minds are still obdurately prejudiced against his work, admirable though it be. Because the best way to overcome a lack of comprehension is to accept it as sincere and try to understand it.

The principal charge brought against Dostoevsky in the name of our Western-European logic has been, I think, the irrational, irresolute, and often irresponsible nature of his characters, everything in their appearance that could seem grotesque and wild. It is not, so people aver, real life that he unfolds, but nightmares. In my belief this is utterly mistaken; but let us grant the truth of it for argument's sake, and refrain from answering after the manner of Freud that there is more sincerity in our dream-life than in the actions of our real existence. Hear rather what Dostoevsky has to say for himself on the subject of dreams:

> These obvious absurdities and impossibilities with which your dream was overflowing... you accepted all at once, almost without the slightest surprise, at the very time when, on another side, your reason was at its highest tension and showed extraordinary power, cunning, sagacity, and logic. And why, too, on waking and fully returning to reality, do you feel almost every time, and sometimes with extraordinary intensity, that you have left something unexplained behind with the dream, and at the same time you feel that interwoven with these absurdities some thought lies hidden, and a thought that is real, something belonging to your actual life, something that exists and always has existed in your heart. It's as though something new, prophetic, that you were awaiting, has been told you in your dream. [*The Idiot* (1868–1869)]

What Dostoevsky says here about dreams we shall apply to his own books, not for a moment that I would consider assimilating these stories to the absurdities of certain dreams, because we feel when we leave one of his books, even should our reason refuse complete agreement with it, that he has laid his finger on some obscure spot "which is part of our actual life." In this, I think, we shall find explained the refusal of certain minds, in the name of Western-European civilization, to admit Dostoevsky's genius, because I readily observe that in all our Western literature (and I do not limit myself to French alone) the novel, with but rare exceptions, concerns itself solely with relations between man and man, passion and intellect, with family, social, and class relations, but never, practically never with the relations between the individual and his self or his God, which are to Dostoevsky all important....

AN EXPLORATION OF THE INNER LIFE

The miracle Dostoevsky accomplished consists in this: each of his characters—and he created a world of them—lives by virtue of his own personality, and these intimately personal beings, each with his peculiar secret, are introduced to us in all their puzzling complexity. The wonder of it is that the problems are lived over by each of his characters, or rather let us say the problems exist at the expense of his characters: problems which conflict, struggle, and assume human guise or triumph before our eyes.

No question is too transcendent for Dostoevsky to handle

in one of his novels; but, having said this, I am bound at once
to add that he never approaches a question from the abstract, ideas never exist for him but as functions of his characters, wherein lies their perpetual relativity and source of
power. One individual evolves a certain theory concerning
God, providence, and life eternal because he knows he must
die in a few days' time, in a few hours maybe (Ippolit in *The
Idiot*): another (in *The Possessed*) builds up an entire system
of metaphysics, containing Nietzsche in embryo, on the
premise of self-destruction, for in a quarter of an hour he is
going to take his own life, and hearing him speak, it is impossible to distinguish whether his philosophy postulates
his suicide or his suicide his philosophy. Prince Myshkin [in
The Idiot] owes his most wonderful, most heavenly raptures
to the imminence of an epileptic fit. In conclusion I have
only one comment to offer: though pregnant with thought,
Dostoevsky's novels are never abstract, indeed, of all the
books I know, they are the most palpitating with life.

Representative as Dostoevsky's characters are, they never
seem to forsake their humanity to become mere symbols or
the types familiar in our classical drama. They keep their
individuality which is as specific as in Dickens's most peculiar creations, and as powerfully drawn and painted as any
portrait in any literature.

Dostoyevsky's Themes Are Epic and Tragic

Vyacheslav Ivanov

Translated from the Russian, this essay first
appeared in Oxford, England, as part of a book-
length historical study. In it, scholar Vyacheslav
Ivanov examines Dostoyevsky's novels for their tragic
aspects. Ivanov makes comparisons between books
such as the ninth century B.C. Homeric epics *The
Odyssey* and *The Iliad* to Dostoyevsky's more
complex tragic novels. By comparing Dostoyevsky's
work with that of the ancient playwright Aeschylus,
Ivanov shows how Dostoyevsky refused to be content
with "idle musings." Though influenced by the story-
telling of the English writer Charles Dickens and the
French writer Honoré de Balzac, Dostoyevsky wove
his stories into tragedies, a break with the happy
endings that had become expected in novels.

What strikes us at the first glance in Dostoevsky's work is
the very close approximation of the novel-form to the prototype of tragedy. It is not as if he had deliberately, and for
artistic reasons, striven for this approximation. On the contrary, he arrived at it accidentally and in all simplicity. His
whole being demanded it. He could create in no other way,
because in no other way could he achieve either an intellectual conception or an artist's vision of life. The inner structure of his creative genius was tragic.

Thus it came about, entirely of itself, that whatever Dostoevsky had to express in his epic-narrative style (he never
attempted to write a play: the limitations of the stage were
obviously too narrow for him) was shaped—both in whole
and in part, and of inward necessity—to conform with the
laws of tragedy. His work is the most striking example we
know of the identity of form and content—insofar as by con-

Excerpted from "The Novel—Tragedy," in *Freedom and the Tragic Life: A Study in Dostoevsky* by Vyacheslav Ivanov, translated by Norman Cameron. Translation copyright
©1957 by Farrar, Straus & Giroux, Inc. Reprinted by permission of Farrar, Straus &
Giroux.

tent we mean the original intuitive perception of life, and by form the means of transmuting this by art into the flesh and blood of a new world of living entities.

Aeschylus said of himself that his works were only the crumbs from Homer's feast. The *Iliad* emerged, as the first and greatest of tragedies, at a time when there could be no question of tragedy as an art-form. Chronologically the oldest, and in its perfection the incomparable, monument of the European epic, the *Iliad* is essentially a tragedy as much in its general conception and in the development of its action, as in the pathos that informs it. According to an ancient definition, the *Iliad* is, in contradistinction to the "ethical" *Odyssey,* a "pathetic" poem—that is to say, a poem that portrays the sorrows and woes of its heroes. In the *Odyssey* the tragic tension which till then was the basic element of epic poetry has already been exhausted; and from this point onwards there begins a slow decline of the heroic epic in general.

The novel-form, on the other hand, has developed in a contrary direction. In modern times it has evolved with ever greater power and impact, becoming ever more many-sided and comprehensive, until finally, in its urge to acquire the characteristics of great art, it has become capable of conveying pure tragedy.

THE EPIC AND THE NOVEL DESCRIBED

Plato described the epic as a hybrid, or mixed, form, partly narrative or instructive, partly mimetic or dramatic—the latter in those passages where the narration is interrupted with numerous and extensive monologues or dialogues, by the characters, whose words reach us in *oratio recta,* directly from the mouths of the masks that the poet has conjured into existence upon the imaginary tragic stage. Plato concludes that, on the one hand, lyrical or epic-lyrical enunciations (expressing what the poet says in his own person), and, on the other hand, the drama (comprising everything that the poet relates word for word as authentic sayings of his heroes) are two natural and clearly distinct forms of poetry; whereas the epic combines in itself both lyrical and dramatic elements. This dual nature of the epic, as it was recognized by Plato, may be explained on the assumption that it arose from the conglomerate art of ancient times—the art described by Alexander Veselovsky, and defined by him as "syncretic"—in which the epic was not yet distinguished from ritual musical performances and imitative masked plays. Be that as it may, the tragic element in the *Iliad*—its substance and internal form—is our historical reason for regarding the novel-tragedy not as a decadent form of the purely epic romance, but as an enrichment of it; as the reinstatement of the epic in the full inheritance of its rights. And what entitles us to apply the term "novel-tragedy" to the novels of Dostoevsky is, above all, their basic conception, which is thoroughly and essentially tragic.

HOMER'S INFLUENCE

This excerpt from Dostoyevsky's private notebooks shows the influence of Homer's Iliad. *As a young man, Dostoyevsky wrote to his brother Mikhail, "In* The Iliad, *Homer gave the ancient world an organization to life which is both spiritual and earthly in the sense as Christ gave one to the new world."*

The Iliad is an epic poem of a life so powerful, so full, of such a high moment in the life of a people and, let us note once more, of the life of such a great race that in our time, a time of aspirations, struggles, doubts, faith (for our time is a time of faith), in a word, in our time of a more intense life, this universal harmony incarnated by the *Iliad* can act on the soul in the most decisive fashion.

"The joy of the story-teller"—the self-sufficing pleasure in invention of adventures and surprising entanglements, in the many-coloured tapestry of overlapping and interlocking situations—at one time this was the novelist's professed main object. And it seemed that in this pleasure the epic narrator could find himself entirely anew: carefree, loquacious, inexhaustibly inventive, without any particular desire—or, indeed, real ability—to find the moral of his story. Always he remained loyal to his old predisposition to bring the tale to a happy ending: an ending that would fully satisfy the sympathies aroused in us by our continual participation in the good and ill luck of the hero, and would bring us, after lengthy journeys on the flying carpet, back home to our customary surroundings—leaving us sated with the rich diversity of life mirrored in the bright phantasmagoria of the threshold between reality and dream, and at the same time filled with a healthy hunger for new experiences in our own existence. The enchantment of this "idle musing" is, of course, irrevocably lost to our overclouded and restless epoch. Besides, some vigorous offshoots had branched away from the main stem of the post-medieval novel-literature: the humorous and satiric stories, the didactic or utopian narrative, and, last but not least, since Boccaccio's *Fiametta*, the sentimental love-tale.

INTRICATE TALES OF CATASTROPHE

Nevertheless, the story-teller's art survived, and continued to exploit its flexible, accommodating technique, its own natural wealth of unexpected events, their puzzling complexities and the art of holding the reader in suspense as he awaits the unravelment of an apparently hopeless tangle: and all this Dostoevsky refused to renounce—as also did Balzac and Dickens, who notably influenced him—and he was right to do so. In his case, however, this motley material is subordinated to a special and higher architectural purpose: in all its component parts, however insignificant they may seem, it subserves the construction of a unified tragedy.

In the circumstantial and seemingly exaggerated matter-of-factness of Dostoevsky's style no detail however small may be omitted: so closely do all particulars of the action cohere to the unity of the successive episodes of the story—separated though these are by numerous discursive passages. These episodes, in turn, are worked into the shape of acts, so to speak, in a continually unfolding drama; and these acts, finally, represent in their sequence the iron links of a chain of logic—on which, like a planetary body, hangs the main event which was from the beginning the theme and purpose of the whole work, with all the weight of its contentual and solemn significance; for in this planetary sphere Ormuzd and Ahriman have again matched themselves in battle, and the work has found its own Apocalypse, its own Day of Judgement.

CHAPTER 2

Crime and Punishment

READINGS ON
FYODOR DOSTOYEVSKY

Crime and Punishment's Continuous Flow of Time

Philip Rahv

Philip Rahv, a Russian-born intellectual and political theorist, borrowed his ideas of time and movement from the French novelist Marcel Proust and the French philosopher Henri Bergson. In the following passage, originally published in *Partisan Review,* a magazine Rahv edited in the United States, Bergson's theory of *durée réelle* (the continuous flow of time) is used to describe the action, or movement of plot, of *Crime and Punishment.* Because narrator Raskolnikov's memory, or consciousness, appears inseparable from the actual past or present of the novel, virtually every moment of *Crime and Punishment* is linked to a single event—the murder of the old pawnbroker. This event, which occurs in an incredibly short space of time, is foreshadowed, lived, or recalled in nearly every moment of the novel. Thus the novel is an illustration of one moment continuously flowing into the past, the present, and the future.

Is [*Crime and Punishment*] the type of narrative nowadays called a psycho-thriller? Yes, in a sense it is, being above all, in its author's own words, the psychological account of a crime. The crime is murder. But in itself this is in no way exceptional, for the very same crime occurs in nearly all of Dostoevsky's novels. Proust once suggested grouping them together under a single comprehensive title: *The Story of a Crime.*

Where this novel differs, however, from the works following it is in the totality of its concentration on that obsessive theme. Virtually everything in the story turns on Raskolnikov's murder of the old pawnbroker and her sister Lizaveta, and it is this concentration which makes the novel so

From Philip Rahv, "Dostoevsky in *Crime and Punishment,*" *Partisan Review,* vol. 27 (1960), 393–425, ©1960 by Philip Rahv. Reprinted by permission of Betty Rahv for the estate of the author.

fine an example of artistic economy and structural cohesion. Free of distractions of theme and idea, and with no confusing excess or over-ingenuity in the manipulation of the plot, such as vitiates the design of *A Raw Youth* and reduces the impact of *The Idiot*, *Crime and Punishment* is the one novel of Dostoevsky's in which his powerful appeal to our intellectual interests is most directly and naturally linked to the action.

The superiority of this work in point of structure has been repeatedly remarked upon, but what has not been sufficiently noted is its extraordinary narrative pace. Consider the movement of Part I, for instance. In this comparatively short section (coming to eighty-four pages in Constance Garnett's translation), we get to know the protagonist fairly well, to know the conditions of crushing poverty and isolation under which he lives and the complex origins of his "loathsome scheme"; we see him going through a rehearsal-visit to the victim's flat; we listen to Marmeladov's sermon in the pothouse, to the recital of his domestic woes, including the circumstances that forced his daughter Sonya to become a prostitute; we witness the drunken old man's home-coming and the hysterical violence with which he is received by his wife; then we read with Raskolnikov the long letter from his mother, learning a good deal about his family situation; we dream with him the frightful dream, looking at once to the past and to the future, of the beating to death of the little mare; finally, after several more scenes of the strictest dramatic relevance, we are brought to a close-up of the double murder, probably the most astonishing description of its kind in fiction, and watch the murderer returning to his lodgings where, after putting back the axe under the porter's bench, he climbs the stairs to sink on his bed in blank forgetfulness.

Thus in this first section of seven chapters a huge quantity of experience is qualitatively organized, with the requisite information concerning the hero's background driven into place through a consummate use of the novelistic device of foreshortening, and with the swift narrative tempo serving precisely as the prime means of controlling and rendering credible the wild queerness of what has been recounted. For this wild queerness cannot be made to yield to explanation or extrinsic analysis. To gain our consent—to enlist, that is, our poetic faith—the author must either dramatize or perish, and for full success he must proceed with the dramatic representation at a pace producing an effect of virtual instantaneousness. To have secured this effect is a triumph of Dostoevsky's creative method—a triumph because the instantaneous is a quality of Being rather than of mind and not open to question. As the vain efforts of so many philosophers have demonstrated, Being is irreducible to the categories of explanation or interpretation.

A STRICTLY FUNCTIONAL PLOT

The artistic economy, force and tempo of Part I is sustained throughout the novel. (The epilogue, in which hope and belief play havoc with the imaginative logic of the work, is something else again.) There is no wasted detail in it, none that can be shown to be functionally inoperative in advancing the action and our insight into its human agents. And it is important to observe that the attaining of this fullness and intensity of representation is conditional upon Dostoevsky's capacity to subdue the time element of the story to his creative purpose. Readers not deliberately attentive to the time-lapse of the action are surprised to learn that its entire span is only two weeks and that of Part I only three days. Actually, there is no real lapse of time in the story because we are virtually unaware of it apart from the tension of the rendered experience. Instead of time lapsing there is the concrete flow of duration contracting and expanding with the rhythm of the dramatic movement.

Least of all is it a chronological frame that time provides in this novel. As the Russian critic K. Mochulsky has so aptly remarked, its time is purely psychological, a function of human consciousness, in other words the very incarnation of Bergson's *durée réelle*. And it is only in Bergsonian terms that one can do it justice. Truly, Dostoevsky succeeds here in converting time into a kind of progress of Raskolnikov's mental state, which is not actually a state but a process of incessant change eating into the future and expanding with the duration it accumulates, like a snowball growing larger as it rolls upon itself, to use Bergson's original image.

This effect is partly accomplished by the exclusion from Raskolnikov's consciousness of everything not directly pertaining to his immediate situation. From beginning to end he is in a state of crisis from which there is no diversion or escape either in memory or fantasy. The import of what he thinks, feels, and remembers is strictly functional to the present. Thus he thinks of his mother, who is involved in the action, with distinct alternations of feelings, while his dead father hardly exists for him. He belongs to the past, and so far as Raskolnikov is concerned the past is empty of affect. The one time he evokes his father's figure is in the anguished dream of the beating to death of the little mare, and his appearance in that dream is singularly passive, manifestly carrying with it no charge of emotion. This dream, enacting a tragic catharsis, is introduced with calculated ambiguity. Is the dreamer actually remembering an episode of his childhood or is he imagining the memory? In any case, though the dream is of the past its meaning is all in the present. The pitiful little mare, whipped across the eyes and butchered by Mikolka and a crowd of rowdy peasants, stands for all such victims of life's insensate cruelty, in particular such victims as Sonya and Lizaveta whose appeal to Raskolnikov is that of "poor gentle things . . . whose eyes are soft and gentle." Also, the mare stands above all for Raskolnikov himself, and in embracing her bleeding head in a frenzy of compassion it is himself he is embracing, bewailing, consoling. He is present in the dream not only as the little boy witnessing an act of intolerable brutality but as at once its perpetrator and victim too. The dream's imagery is entirely prospective in that it points ahead, anticipating the murder Raskolnikov is plotting even while exposing it as an act of self-murder. Its latent thought-content is a warning that in killing the pawnbroker he would be killing himself too, and it is indeed in this light that he understands his deed afterwards when, in confessing to Sonya, he cries out: "Did I murder the old woman? I murdered myself, not her! I crushed myself once and for all, forever." The cathartic effect of the dream is such that upon awakening he recovers the sense of his human reality, feeling "as though an abscess that had been forming in his heart had suddenly broken . . . he was free from that spell, that sorcery, that obsession." But the catharsis is momentary, and he no sooner hears that the pawnbroker will be alone in her flat the next evening than he is again gripped by his obsession.

Guilt in *Crime and Punishment*

Alfred L. Bem

In this look at *Crime and Punishment*, originally published in Berlin in 1938, Russian scholar Alfred L.
Bem makes use of Dostoyevsky's personal notebooks
and early sketches to show the novelist's fascination
with the motives behind the criminal mind. It was
Dostoyevsky's opinion, Bem asserts, that a criminal's
feelings of discomfort and remorse are often connected not to any actual crime, but to a preconceived
notion of guilt. Feelings of shame and guilt, Dostoyevsky believed, may even precede a criminal act.

It is often said that Dostoevsky's "novel-tragedy" gravitates
toward a single major "catastrophic" event, one usually connected with a crime; what has not been sufficiently stressed
is that Dostoevsky's focus is not crime at all, but its corol-
lary—guilt. . . . We shall not be concerned here with any objective norms of guilt and crime, but only with those psychological substrata on which these norms rest. . . . Crime
will be understood only as the *awareness by the subject himself of some moral norm which he has violated*, quite apart
from whether this violation has been recognized externally,
morally, as a real crime. Without such a limitation [in the
definition of crime] the correlation between guilt and crime,
which plays such a crucial role in Dostoevsky, would be incomprehensible. Quite often, particularly in Dostoevsky's
earlier works, the feeling of guilt becomes extremely and
even tragically intense when only an extremely vague sense
of a concrete crime lends support to this feeling. In other
words, the objective crime which awakens a feeling of guilt
may turn out to be so insignificant as to provide no explanation for the intense feeling of guilt. In this case the tragedy of
guilt can be understood and disclosed only by presupposing

From Alfred L. Bem, "The Problem of Guilt," in *Twentieth-Century Interpretations of
Crime and Punishment*, translated and edited by Robert Louis Jackson (Englewood
Cliffs, NJ: Prentice-Hall, 1974). Reprinted by permission of Robert Louis Jackson. Sub-
headings in this reprint have been added by Greenhaven editors.

that the *concrete crime serves as a surrogate for some crime not openly manifested yet present in the psyche*, like a trauma or pressure of conscience.

To understand Dostoevsky's thought one must allow for the presence in the human psyche of a feeling of sinfulness as such, independent of the existence of any concrete crime— what we might call *the feeling of original sin....* We can assume, then, that the feeling of sin, of guilt can be present in the psyche unaccompanied by any consciousness of crime. Indeed, the guilt-ridden consciousness often seeks a crime, as though it wished to free itself from an overwhelming sense of fatality and enter the world of ordinary human criminality, apparently more tolerable to human consciousness than the intense pressure of metaphysical sinfulness. It is only here that we can find an explanation for Dostoevsky's idea that "each of us is guilty for all," and for his characteristic notion of the "desire to suffer." With the latter in mind we can turn to the episode in *Crime and Punishment* with the house painter Mikolka, the workman who takes on himself Raskolnikov's crime. The episode is a minor one, but of central importance for our theme.

MIKOLKA'S CONFESSION

No one first meeting the painter Mikolka Dementiev suspected in him a spiritual complexity which would lead to his puzzling assumption of guilt for the murder of the old lady. We find an ingenuous, life-loving lad, with a taste for the bottle. Porfiry Petrovich, a man not without insight, characterizes him this way:

> First he's immature, still a child; and not that he's a coward, but sensitive, a kind of artist type. Yes, really. You mustn't laugh at me for explaining him like that. He is innocent and completely impressionable. He has feelings; he is a fantast. He can sing and dance, and they say he can tell stories so people gather from all around to listen. And he'll go to school and he'll laugh himself silly because somebody somehow crooked a finger at him; and he'll drink himself senseless, not because he's a drunkard, but just every now and then, when people buy him drinks; he's like a child still.

This characterization tallies completely with our first impression of the house painters on the day of the murder. The witnesses unanimously testified that there was nothing suspicious in their conduct. Both painters, Nikolai and Dmitri, ran out of the courtyard and began to pummel each other in fun. . . . How is it possible that this apparently simple person could come to take on himself somebody else's crime? This psychological enigma must be solved, and Dostoevsky does so; but as usual when a psychological explanation is to be found in the unconscious, Dostoevsky provides an explanation on a conscious level: in this case, introducing the motif of "fear" that he, Mikolka, would be convicted. This fear overcomes Mikolka when he learns about the murder of the old lady and feels guilty because he had picked up the earrings dropped by the murderer; his fear of being accused became unbearable and he wants to hang himself. Dostoevsky tries to give the reader a convincing explanation of Mikolka's behavior by making us aware of Mikolka's internal distress; but he does not yet make it clear to us why Mikolka decided to assume somebody else's guilt. Porfiry Petrovich hints at the reason for this strange behavior; he suggests that the explanation must be sought elsewhere in Mikolka's moral experiences. The house painter turns out not to be so spiritually uncomplicated as we had imagined; he has his own enigmatic past. Porfiry Petrovich observes:

> But did you know that he was a Raskolnik? Well, not a Raskolnik, exactly, but a member of one of those religious sects. There were members of his family who were Runners; they'd run away from wordly involvement. He himself actually spent two years, not long ago, under the spiritual tutelage of some holy elder in some village. . . . He himself was moved to run off into the wilderness! He had the spirit, would pray to God at night, read the old "true" books and reread them, for hours on end. . . . Well, now, in jail it seems he remembered the honorable elder, and the Bible turned up again, too. Do you know what they mean, Rodion Romanych, when they talk of "taking suffering upon themselves?" They don't mean suffering for anybody in particular, just "one has to suffer." That means, *accept* suffering; and if it's from the authorities, so much the better. . . . You mean you won't admit that our people produce fantastic characters of this sort? Yes, many. Now the elder is beginning to have some effect again, especially after that business with the noose.

The way was clearly prepared for Mikolka's "fantastic" behavior. The news of the murder which had so disconcerted him and led him to attempt suicide was only the most immediate cause which brought to the surface those feelings of guilt that were hidden in the depths of his unconscious.

Precisely the problem of guilt lay at the root of Mikolka's act, not a superficial "fear" of conviction; indeed, Dostoevsky originally had no intention at all of introducing the latter motive. Twice in the notebooks to the novel he stresses the basic "religious" motive in Mikolka's behavior. Thus, in one part of the manuscript we read: "A workman testifies against himself (he had got caught up with religion), wanted to suffer (but gets muddled). They start pressuring him. And an old man sits there: one has to suffer, he says." A brief note appears in another place. "News at the gathering that a man (a workman) was taken by religion."

We can see from these notes that the root of Mikolka's behavior lay in a "religious" feeling linked with his moral experiences. The fact that Dostoevsky associates these elements in Mikolka's consciousness with the influence of some old religious sectarian serving a prison term with him testifies to Dostoevsky's artistic awareness. Such views on the primordial sinfulness of man were widespread in Russian sectarian religious thought.

One might suspect Dostoevsky of using the whole Mikolka episode only as an artful manoeuvre in the development of a detective story, a way of mixing the cards and holding back the denouement. But his supreme artistry is revealed in another way: concerned with narrative technique, he nevertheless introduces instead of a shallow plot device an incident which is closely connected with the central idea of the novel—the problem of guilt. The house painter, in contradistinction to Raskolnikov who strives to evade responsibility before his conscience for his sin, assumes responsibility for a crime that he did not commit. The interplay between these two responses to the problem of guilt will become even clearer after we examine Raskolnikov's crime.

Mikolka, according to Dostoevsky, "got caught up with religion" under the influence of an old religious sectarian; but in order to get caught up on religion he must have had some spiritual motivation. We must therefore assume a feeling of general sinfulness, of primordial guilt in the depths of Mikolka's consciousness, or, more accurately, in his unconscious—a feeling which sought expression in taking suffering upon himself. The "desire to suffer" cannot be explained without the supposition that there is a primordial feeling of guilt, the experience of primordial sinfulness, at the basis of the human soul. The incident involving Mikolka in *Crime and Punishment* is only an artistic expression of this phenomenon observed by Dostoevsky in the depths of his own being. . . .

AN INTELLECTUAL JUSTIFICATION FOR CRIME

Raskolnikov, a prisoner of his *idée fixe* [obsession], kills an old money lender. The whole novel is built around the unique process of disintegration in the hero's soul: his intellectual life is split off from the life of feeling. I do not know how I can express my thought more precisely here. A state of spiritual unity and harmony gives way to a "disintegration" in which one aspect of a person's being becomes overextended and eclipses the rest. But though driven into the unconscious these other aspects of self can remain active there and affect conduct in a special way. It is still possible then, paradoxically, for a criminal in his acts to preserve some inner nobility: just this inner split in Raskolnikov is the content of *Crime and Punishment.*

Crime is presented here as an unquestioned fact, not only in the formal but also the moral sense. But this fact does not penetrate Raskolnikov's consciousness; it takes the form in his unconscious of a potential power of conscience. To the very end, mind remains unrepentant. Even in prison, after his conviction, Raskolnikov still holds inflexibly to the idea that the murder is justifiable. And yet his whole being, his entire moral nature is shaken precisely by the moral aspect of the murder. Like a shadow, Sonia continually follows him and directs him onto the path of repentance. Dostoevsky portrays this symbolic role of Sonia with amazing power. When Raskolnikov wavers in his decision to confess, Sonia at that very moment is with him as his embodied conscience. As he leaves the police station he sees her:

> There, not far from the gate, stood Sonia, numb and deathly pale; and she looked at him with a wild look. He stopped before her. There was something painful and tortured in her face, something desperate. She threw up her hands. A ghastly, lost smile forced its way to his lips. He stood there and grinned. Then he turned back upstairs to the station.

His fate is decided: he confesses to killing the old woman.

Here, then, is an extraordinary situation: in the absence of any conscious guilt feeling, guilt is not only subconsciously present but even determines the final outcome of the spiritual drama. Thus, Dostoevsky is right when he envisages the possibility, too, of Raskolnikov's spiritual resurrection, that is, the restoration of his spiritual unity.

Tobacco and Alcohol in *Crime and Punishment*

Leo Tolstoy

Count Leo Tolstoy was a contemporary of Dostoyevsky's. His novels *War and Peace* and *Anna Karenina*
are considered classics of world literature. A political
activist, ethical philosopher, and religious reformer,
Tolstoy's essays were influential in Russia and the
West. In this essay originally entitled "Why Do Men
Stupefy Themselves?", Tolstoy uses *Crime and Punishment*'s Raskolnikov to illustrate how the ingestion of
even mild drugs can have disastrous consequences.

But can such a small—such a trifling—alteration as the
slight intoxication produced by the moderate use of wine or
tobacco produce important consequences? "If a man smokes
opium or hashish, or intoxicates himself with wine till he
falls down and loses his senses, of course the consequences
may be very serious; but it surely cannot have any serious
consequences if a man merely comes slightly under the influence of hops or tobacco," is what is usually said. It seems
to people that a slight stupefaction, a little darkening of the
judgement, cannot have any important influence. But to
think so is like supposing that it may harm a watch to be
struck against a stone, but that a little dirt introduced into it
cannot be harmful.

Remember, however, that the chief work actuating man's
whole life is not done by his hands, his feet, or his back, but
by his consciousness. Before a man can do anything with his
feet or hands, a certain alteration has first to take place in
his consciousness. And this alteration defines all the subsequent movements of the man. Yet these alterations are always minute and almost imperceptible.

[The celebrated Russian painter, K.P.] Bryullóv one day
corrected a pupil's study. The pupil glanced at the altered

From Leo Tolstoy, "Why Do Men Stupefy Themselves?" in *Recollections and Essays*,
translated by Aylmer Maude (Oxford: Oxford University Press, 1937). Reprinted by permission of Oxford University Press.

drawing, exclaimed: "Why, you only touched it a tiny bit, but it is quite another thing." Bryullóv replied: "Art begins where the tiny bit begins."

That saying is strikingly true not only of art but of all life. One may say that true life begins where the tiny bit begins— where what seem to us minute and infinitely small alterations take place. True life is not lived where great external changes take place—where people move about, clash, fight, and slay one another—it is lived only where these tiny, tiny, infinitesimally small changes occur.

RASKÓLNIKOV'S ALTERED CONSCIOUSNESS

Raskólnikov did not live his true life when he murdered the old woman or her sister. When murdering the old woman herself, and still more when murdering her sister, he did not live his true life, but acted like a machine, doing what he could not help doing—discharging the cartridge with which he had long been loaded. One old woman was killed, another stood before him, the axe was in his hand.

Raskólnikov lived his true life not when he met the old woman's sister, but at the time when he had not yet killed any old woman, nor entered a stranger's lodging with intent to kill, nor held the axe in his hand, nor had the loop in his overcoat by which the axe hung. He lived his true life when he was lying on the sofa in his room, deliberating not at all about the old woman, nor even as to whether it is or is not permissible at the will of one man to wipe from the face of the earth another, unnecessary and harmful, man, but whether he ought to live in Petersburg or not, whether he ought to accept money from his mother or not, and on other questions not at all relating to the old woman. And then—in that region quite independent of animal activities—the question whether he would or would not kill the old woman was decided. That question was decided—not when, having killed one old woman, he stood before another, axe in hand—but when he was doing nothing and was only thinking, when only his consciousness was active: and in that consciousness tiny, tiny alterations were taking place. It is at such times that one needs the greatest clearness to decide correctly the questions that have arisen, and it is just then that one glass of beer, or one cigarette, may prevent the solution of the question, may postpone the decision, stifle the voice of conscience and prompt a decision of the question in favour of the lower,

DRUNKENNESS

In this excerpt from a letter to a friend, A.A. Krayevsky,
Dostoyevsky describes the novel that would later become
Crime and Punishment. *He refers to it here by its earlier title—*
The Drunkards.

My novel is called *The Drunkards* and will be tied in with the
current issue of drunkenness. Not only is the problem of
drunkenness analyzed, but all its ramifications are shown, especially scenes of family life and the education of children in
such conditions, etc. etc.

animal nature—as was the case with Raskólnikov

Tiny, tiny alterations—but on them depend the most im-
mense and terrible consequences. Many material changes
may result from what happens when a man has taken a decision and begun to act: houses, riches, and people's bodies
may perish, but nothing more important can happen than
what was hidden in the man's consciousness. The limits of
what can happen are set by consciousness.

And boundless results of unimaginable importance may
follow from most minute alterations occurring in the do-
main of consciousness.

A WARNING FOR READERS

Do not let it be supposed that what I am saying has anything
to do with the question of free will or determinism. Discussion on that question is superfluous for my purpose, or for
any other for that matter. Without deciding the question
whether a man can, or cannot, act as he wishes (a question
in my opinion not correctly stated), I am merely saying that
since human activity is conditioned by infinitesimal alterations in consciousness, it follows (no matter whether we
admit the existence of free will or not) that we must pay particular attention to the condition in which these minute alterations take place, just as one must be specially attentive
to the condition of scales on which other things are to be
weighed. We must, as far as it depends on us, try to put ourselves and others in conditions which will not disturb the
clearness and delicacy of thought necessary for the correct
working of conscience, and must not act in the contrary
manner—trying to hinder and confuse the work of conscience by the use of stupefying substances.

For man is a spiritual as well as an animal being. He may be moved by things that influence his spiritual nature, or by things that influence his animal nature, as a clock may be moved by its hands or by its main wheel. And just as it is best to regulate the movement of a clock by means of its inner mechanism, so a man—oneself or another—is best regulated by means of his consciousness. And as with a clock one has to take special care of that part by means of which one can best move the inner mechanism, so with a man one must take special care of the cleanness and clearness of consciousness which is the thing that best moves the whole man. To doubt this is impossible; everyone knows it. But a need to deceive oneself arises. People are not as anxious that consciousness should work correctly as they are that it should seem to them that what they are doing is right, and they deliberately make use of substances that disturb the proper working of their consciousness.

Four Dreams in *Crime and Punishment*

Ruth Mortimer

Philology, or the study of written texts, was a subject that interested Ruth Mortimer. In this essay, which first appeared in the United States in 1956, Mortimer skillfully separates one particular aspect of *Crime and Punishment:* the four dreams. Mortimer believes that analyzing the dreams gives the reader clues to understanding Dostoyevsky's key themes. After carefully locating each dream within the novel, Mortimer then discusses the significance of each dream and compares them to one another.

[In *Crime and Punishment,* there] are four fully told dreams which concern the chief character, Raskolnikov. Each of these dreams leads into the next, illustrating both the significance of the dream in the complex psychology of a character like Raskolnikov and the use of the dream for dramatic atmosphere. In creating these dreams, Dostoevski has repeated events or reshaped ideas in terms of the unconscious of the character who is dreaming. Thus the succession of dreams forms a psychic pattern of motivation as valid as the course of external episodes.

The novel, as all its readers know, is centered around Raskolnikov's theory of the self-willed criminal, the extraordinary man, the Napoleon, who has a right to transgress the laws of ordinary men in order to carry out an idea. The test of this theory, the proof that Raskolnikov himself is one of these extraordinary men, is to be the murder of an old pawnbroker, and the novel opens with an experimental visit to the old woman's flat. The first four scenes of the book [the visit to the pawnbroker's flat; the meeting with Marmeladov; the letter from Raskolnikov's mother; the encounter with the drunken girl] form the substance of the first dream.

From Ruth Mortimer, "Dostoevski and the Dream," *Modern Philology,* vol. 54, no. 2, November 1956, pp. 106–16. Copyright ©1956 by The University of Chicago. Reprinted by permission of the University of Chicago Press.

THE DREAM OF THE MARE

The four . . . scenes are associated in Raskolnikov's mind by the conscious theme, the state of poverty and degradation into which he has fallen. He counts his money, reckoning the kopecks given to the Marmeladovs, to the servant Nastasya for his mother's letter, and to the policemen, all taken from the amount which the old pawnbroker had just given him in exchange for his father's watch. Thus are they linked by purely mechanical means. That they have another, an implicit, connection is evident from the mode of their convergence and translation into the dream of the beaten horse.

This dream in outline moves swiftly. Raskolnikov as a child is accompanying his father to a requiem service for his grandmother and a visit to the grave of his brother. The road to the church runs past a tavern, and there the child is frightened by the rough sport of a group of drunken peasants. Outside the tavern stands a heavy cart with a mare, "a thin little sorrel beast," in the shafts. Mikolka, the owner of the cart, calls to his friends to get in, so that the mare can pull them all. When he finds that the horse cannot move the heavy load, he and his comrades beat her to death before the eyes of the child Raskolnikov. Not until the mare has been brutally killed with whips and crowbars before the grief-stricken child, does Raskolnikov awaken from this violent nightmare.

From the desperate confusion of his adult life, Raskolnikov has returned in this dream to his childhood, to the town of his birth, in order to find again the same security of that time so recently recalled to him by his mother's letter. The letter closed with the words, "Remember . . . when your father was living . . . how happy we all were in those days." This last sentence had taken hold of Raskolnikov; but the unconscious attempt to relive a moment of that innocent happiness fails, and the childhood experience in the dream evolves as one of intense fear and suffering, from which even his father cannot shield him. The preliminary details of the country landscape—the "grey and heavy day," the town "on a level flat as bare as the hand," the corpse, "a dark blur on the very edge of the horizon," the black dust of the winding road—all create an atmosphere of oppression and foreboding. The grotesque meeting with Marmeladov in the tavern is directly responsible for the dream setting.

Raskolnikov's contemplation of the act of murder means that he has renounced both family ties and early religious training. The dream is a return to both. Raskolnikov is now with his father, whose protection he has lost. In this loss he must feel an additional sense of his own responsibility toward his mother and his sister Dounia. Dounia and his father have a definite symbolic association with the murder. It is the ring which his sister had given him which he takes to the pawnbroker's on his first visit, and it is his father's silver watch which he uses as the excuse for his experimental visit to complete his preparations for the murder.

In a sense, the struggling mare, so ridiculously unsuited to her heavy load, symbolizes a whole class of "sacrificial" women, of whom Raskolnikov's mother is one; but a more specific examination of the details of this part of the dream shows how closely Raskolnikov's meeting with the drunken girl and the stout sensualist on K——Boulevard parallels this scene. At the time he compared the obvious plight of the unknown girl with that of Sonia, "the eternal victim," and of Dounia, at one moment at the mercies of Svidrigailov, at another selling herself to Luzhin as his fiancée. Identified in the dream with the mare, helpless under the primitive passion of her tormentor, these women are translated by Raskolnikov into animals for hire. . . . In the prolonged struggle of the mare is dramatized the senseless suffering and the strange endurance under that suffering of women like Sonia.

A DOUBLE SIGNIFICANCE

Because of the conflict in Raskolnikov's mind, the figures in this dream have a double significance. Behind Mikolka's act of violence lies the larger design of Raskolnikov's intended murder of the old woman. In this context, Mikolka is Raskolnikov himself, and the mare, his victim. Mikolka, warm-blooded, violent, is the opposite of Raskolnikov, the cold theorist; but the act of murder is the same. The peasant's reckless shout, "I feel as if I could kill her," is a direct statement of Raskolnikov's thought displaced into this situation. He hates his victim as Raskolnikov hates the old woman. As he brandishes the axe over the mare, he stands as Raskolnikov has imagined himself standing, administering the blows which receive their strength only from an elemental fury, not from reasoned theories. The cry, "You are not a

Christian," repeatedly rises from the crowd; and throughout his preparations for the murder, Raskolnikov has tortured himself with that same accusation. In the death of the mare Raskolnikov sees the blood of the old woman. Had he examined his theory further, he would have seen that the old woman, once murdered, would be as useless to him as the dead mare to Mikolka, that his aid, little as it might be, would come from the living and not from the dead.

In order to commit murder, Raskolnikov must stop believing both in the power of life and in the horror of violent death. The death scene of the mare is prolonged for two reasons: to define the character of the murderer and to imply the existence of a life-force in the animal which will resist the brutal attack almost to the breaking point of the murderer himself. Extended to the human personality, this resistance may be involuntary. Raskolnikov is a witness, later in the novel, to an unsuccessful suicide attempt, the second failure on the part of a strange and hopeless woman. Or the life-force may be based on spiritual conviction. Sonia, even in despair, will not listen to Raskolnikov's suggestion of suicide as the way out of her responsibilities. Raskolnikov himself cannot take his own life, even in his delirium after the murder. Directly after the murder, he cannot believe in the ease of his own crime; he interrupts his hasty search of the old woman's rooms to make sure she is not still alive.

We have in this dream a tragic comparison of the adult Raskolnikov with the child. One suggestion may be traced back from a statement toward the end of the novel, in the description of a requiem service for Marmeladov's wife, Katerina Ivanovna: "From his childhood the thought of death and the presence of death had something oppressive and mysteriously awful." At the time of the dream, Raskolnikov's waking thoughts revolved around death, the violent death he would inflict upon the old woman. The dream concerns two forms of death, contrasting the ritual of the church service, the solemn peace of the graveyard, with the horrible death of the mare. In the child there is respect even for those whom he does not know; in the mature Raskolnikov the outward isolation and indifference to humanity are frightening. As a child, he loved the church, the ikons, the old priest; as a murderer, he hurriedly drops the old woman's crosses on the body of his victim.

Yet the terror which Raskolnikov experiences as a child

over the death struggles of the helpless mare predicts his loss of control over the act of murder. The early emotions aroused in the dream are still within him. The basic feelings of pity and compassion, natural to the child, must still exist in Raskolnikov if he can suffer them so acutely in a dream. . . . The dream serves as a warning to him, a warning which he partially realizes as he shudders at the recollection but which is yet powerless against the fixation of his theories. He still believes in his motive for the murder, but, unconsciously, he searches for an argument which will invalidate that motive. He is not to be released until he recognizes that there are no rational answers to his questions. In the first moments after the dream, moments of supposed freedom from the obsession of the murder, he prays, "Lord, show me my path—I renounce that accursed . . . dream of mine." But the prayer is an empty prayer, and the word "dream" means not the theory of the murder as Raskolnikov intended it to mean but a fatal renunciation of the child of the beaten-horse dream.

THE DREAM OF THE POLICE OFFICIAL

The second dream, which follows the actual murder, has as its direct stimulus a summons to the police office, a coincidence involving not the expected accusation of murder, but only a charge of nonpayment of an I.O.U. to his landlady. The latent content of the dream is the act of murder. In this dream Raskolnikov starts up in terror at the sound of screams, blows, and curses coming from somewhere outside his room. In a moment he recognizes that the screams are those of his landlady and that her assailant is Ilya Petrovich, the "Explosive Lieutenant" of the police office scene. There is here a return of the fear Raskolnikov had had on facing that official in the police office, a subjective continuation of the beaten-horse dream and also a reflection of the sordid surroundings of his present lodgings, in which such an incident was not unlikely to occur. There is, more significantly, an adaptation of the murder, in which the hot-tempered official takes the place of Raskolnikov himself.

This dream is imaginatively closer to his emotional experience of the crime than is the actual murder scene. There is no conclusion to the last part of this dream and intentionally no sense of Raskolnikov's awakening from it. His terror of revelation and his relief when he is loosed from the trap unharmed, begun in the police office scene, occur periodically throughout the remainder of the novel in a definite series of tensions and releases—with his questioning by Porfiry Petrovitch, his mock confession to the head clerk, Zametov, his fear of the evidence of an unknown informer—of which this dream is only a foreshadowing.

During the fever which follows the dream of Ilya Petrovitch and the landlady, the murder is so far repressed by Raskolnikov that he is aware only that he has forgotten something which he ought to remember. The indirect character of the dream—he is neither a witness to the action nor a participant in it, in spite of his emotional identification—defines this defensive state of mind before its manifestation in his illness. For Raskolnikov, the interval between the second and third dreams, longer than that between the first two, is one of alternate moods of terror and extreme lucidity.

THE DREAM OF THE STRANGER IN A LONG COAT

The third dream is . . . an attempt to relive the murder, and its outline is closely drawn from the two specific scenes, the actual murder scene and Raskolnikov's compulsive return to the flat after it. The immediate stimulus is the accusation from the "man in the long coat," a stranger met on the street, who suddenly turns on Raskolnikov with the words "You are a murderer." Raskolnikov unconsciously reproduces the scene of his crime in a dream in order to place this stranger there, to discover what evidence he might have for his sinister charge. The confusion of this direct dream-return to the murder throws an interesting light upon Raskolnikov's changing attitude toward his act. His uncertainty at the beginning of the dream indicates a clear break in the motivation of the crime. Throughout the first part of the dream, Raskolnikov is not moving of his own accord but is following the stranger to the scene of the murder, attributing to him complete responsibility for the action, as though this dream figure were again a projection of his act, as in the first two dreams. Once Raskolnikov is in the house and on the staircase, however, the stranger, though still leading him, is not seen, and the details begin to draw on other threads of thought.

It is the disappearance of the stranger from the dream at this point which proves that here he is not fundamentally a projection of the murderer but actually Raskolnikov's conscience, stating the accusation and bringing him finally, of his own volition, to re-experience the murder. This dream is concentrated upon Raskolnikov himself performing the act of violence, whereas, in the preceding dreams, the murder was so far repressed that the furious peasant, Mikolka, and Ilya Petrovitch were the assailants. This repression was caused by an unconscious refusal to admit his own crime. The murder dream implies an extremely intricate psychic motivation: at the moment when Raskolnikov is able to recognize his act sufficiently to reproduce it as his own, the final impression is of failure. Here he finds himself incapable of murder, from a purely physical standpoint. Under the blows of the axe, the old woman sits as though made of wood and only laughs at his vicious attempt. The fact, here reduced to its simplest terms, is, in actuality, the growing realization that psychologically Raskolnikov cannot endure the effects of the murder.

Once again the essential dream image has a dual meaning. The old woman, sitting bent double so that Raskolnikov cannot see her face, is not presented in the dream as anything more than a victim.

A DREAM REMEMBERED

The final dream is objectified in several respects. It is not told directly in the novel but is remembered by Raskolnikov as a dream he had had while in the prison hospital in Siberia. Nor did he himself take any active part in it; he seems rather to have observed its progress. Thus it does not involve specific conscious experience and cannot be subjected to the same type of analysis as the preceding dreams. Its purpose is, in a sense, to present the thesis of the novel in slightly different terms. The entire dream is an allegory, with a fairly uncomplicated symbolism. Representing the final stage in Raskolnikov's renunciation of his theory, this dream is indicative also of a new attitude toward life. Raskolnikov has begun, unconsciously, to fit himself into society once more, to think again in terms of humanity. He visualizes the dangers of the extreme relativism which his theory required, dangers not only to society but also to the man of will.

This idea is translated in the final dream into a plague, a disease brought on by an attack of microbes "endowed with intelligence and will." The mad victims of these attacks believe themselves intellectually infallible and in complete

possession of the truth. They cannot understand one another, and they can form no standards of judgment. . . . Only
a few, a chosen people, will be saved from annihilation, and
these will live "to found a new race" and "to renew the
earth." The choice of words in the recollection of this dream
is important. Here are brought together some of the key concepts of the novel and of Dostoevski's work in general: "the
condemned," "the chosen," "intelligence," "will," "the suf-
ferers," "truth."

In a discussion of crime, early in the novel, Dostoevski
writes of Raskolnikov: "It was his conviction that [an]
eclipse of reason and failure of will power attacked a man
like a disease." In the dream his idea is reversed so that "intelligence and will" are the diseases of humanity. Raskolnikov's theory required the division of mankind into material and superior persons, those who merely existed and
those with the will to act. The dream dictates a division also,
but the chosen people are not the rationalists, the frustrated
victims of the plague, but the quiet people like Sonia.

The central theme of these four dreams is that of violence.
Psychologically, each of them effects for Raskolnikov a
catharsis, in a vivid manifestation of the dominant idea from
both his conscious and his unconscious thought, a terrifying
release of primitive forces. Before each such release, he is in
a state of disease and delirium and close to complete loss of
control. There is a constant attempt to shift responsibility, as
though he believed himself incapable of such imaginings.
Unconsciously, however, he is grasping seemingly isolated
threads in these dreams: the sympathy of the child in the
dream of the beaten horse, the awareness of the "crowd" in
the second dream, the projected mockery of his efforts in the
murder dream, the treachery of free will in the dream of the
plague. Touching him at first indirectly, these images approach conscious realization until, in the final dream,
Raskolnikov himself recognizes the means for his spiritual
regeneration. The awakening from the last dream is literally
an awakening from the "dream" of the murder.

Traditional Symbolism in *Crime and Punishment*

George Gibian

Fluent in Russian, George Gibian was instrumental in translating several studies of Dostoyevsky into English. Here Gibian calls upon his knowledge of traditional symbolism to show how Dostoyevsky subtly sends messages to the reader. He argues that by using meaningful images at the proper moment, Dostoyevsky adds contrast and irony to an already intricate storyline. By making use of recurring visual cues, he is able to foreshadow important events such as the confession of Raskolnikov and his ultimate regeneration.

In *Crime and Punishment* the reader, as well as Raskolnikov, must struggle to draw his own conclusions from a work which mirrors the refractory and contradictory materials of life itself, with their admixture of the absurd, repulsive, and grotesque. The oblique presentation of ideas was Dostoevsky's favorite technique. . . .

Traditional symbolism, that is, symbolism which draws on images established by the Christian tradition and on those common in Russian non-Christian, possibly pre-Christian and pagan, folk thought and expression, is an important element in the structure of *Crime and Punishment*. The outstanding strands of symbolic imagery in the novel are those of water, vegetation, sun and air, the resurrection of Lazarus and Christ, and the earth.

WATER

Water is to Dostoevsky a symbol of rebirth and regeneration. It is regarded as such by the positive characters, for whom it is an accompaniment and an indication of the life-giving

Reprinted by permission of the Modern Language Association of America from George Gibian, "Traditional Symbolism in *Crime and Punishment*," *PMLA*, vol. 70, no. 5 (December 1955), pp. 979–96.

forces in the world. By the same token, the significance of water may be the opposite to negative characters. Water holds the terror of death for the corrupt Svidrigaylov, who confirms his depravity by thinking: "Never in my life could I stand water, not even on a landscape painting.". . . Water, instead of being an instrument of life, becomes for him a hateful, avenging menace during the last hours of his life.

When Raskolnikov is under the sway of rationalism and corrupting ways of thinking, this also is indicated by Dostoevsky by attributing to him negative reactions to water similar to those of Svidrigaylov. In Raskolnikov, however, the battle is not definitely lost. A conflict still rages between his former self—which did have contact with other people and understood the beauty of the river, the cathedral (representing the traditional, religious, and emotional forces), and water—and the new, rationalistic self, which is responsible for the murder and for his inner desiccation.

There is still left in Raskolnikov an instinctive reaction to water (and to beauty) as an instrument of life, although this receptivity, which had been full-blown and characteristic of him in his childhood, is now in his student days overlaid by the utilitarian and rationalistic theories. (In contrast to Svidrigaylov, who feels clearly and unequivocally depressed by the contemplation of beauty.) But Raskolnikov also realizes that his trends of thought have banished him, like Cain, from the brotherhood of men and clouded his right and ability to enjoy beauty and the beneficent influences of life symbolized by water; hence his perplexity and conflict.

A cogent expression of the dominant significance of water to Raskolnikov is available in his dream of the oasis: "He kept day-dreaming, and his day-dreams were all so strange: mostly he imagined himself to be somewhere in Africa, in Egypt, in some sort of oasis. The caravan is resting, the camels are lying down peacefully; palms are growing in a circle all around; they are all having their meal, but he is drinking water all the time, straight from a little stream that flowed babbling close by. And it is so cool, and the wonderful, blue, cold water is running over stones of many colors and over such clean sand, which here and there glittered like gold.". . .

The stream here represents Raskolnikov's desire to be saved from his criminal plan. He is attracted by the possibility of a restful, serene life (expressed here, as frequently elsewhere in the novel, by the cluster of images of water, vegetation, and restfulness) which would be very different from the horrible existence (represented in the first dream by the beating of the mare) into which Raskolnikov subconsciously realizes, his life will develop if he perseveres in his determination to kill the pawnbroker.

The dream is the last attempt by his subconscious to hold out to him a way of life opposite to that to which his reason and will have committed him. It is a desperate and unheeded call which he scornfully rejects as a sign of a passing disease. Symbolism of water is the language used to express the conflict; Raskolnikov's reaction to water is a gauge of his inner state.

VEGETATION

Related to the many references to the river and rain, and often closely associated with them, are two other groups of symbolic imagery: that of vegetation (shrubbery, leaves, bushes, flowers, and greenness in general) and that of the sun (and the related images of light and air).

In contrast to the dusty, hot, stifling, and crowded city, a fitting setting for Raskolnikov's oppressive and murderous thoughts, we find, for example, "the greenness and the freshness" of the Petersburg islands. Before the murder, Raskolnikov walked over to them and the "greenness and the freshness at first pleased his tired eyes, used to the dust of the city, to the lime, and the huge, enclosing, confining houses. Here there were no bad smells, no oppressive heat, no taverns. . . . The flowers particularly attracted his attention.". . . He made his way "into some bushes, lay down on the grass and fell asleep at once," and had the dream of the mare and Nikolka. The natural surroundings reawakened in him the feelings of his youth, through which he came close to avoiding his crime and to finding regeneration without having to pass through the cycle of crime and punishment. It is significant that it was in that particular setting that the dream foreshadowing the murder came to him, with the mare standing for the pawnbroker and all the victimized women of the novel, and with Raskolnikov—this time not a tormentor and criminal, but a child-bystander—sympathizing with the victim and wishing to save her.

By the same token, vegetation exercised the opposite effect on Svidrigaylov: it repelled him. In the inn on the night of his suicide, when he heard the leaves in the garden under his window, he thought, "How I hate the noise of trees at night in a storm and in darkness.". . . The forces symbolic of new life, vegetation as well as rain, either became hateful to him or were perverted by him to serve his destructive purposes, just as he had abused all the relationships of his life: in marriage giving hate instead of love, in presents to his fiancée aiming at causing embarrassment and shock instead of pleasure, and in his relations with his servant domineering and bullying instead of guiding.

Svidrigaylov's perversion of instruments of life is manifested in his dream of the fourteen-year-old girl whom he had driven to suicide—significantly, to suicide by drowning. He first dreams of a profusion of flowers. . . . The flowers suggest the last outburst of his craving for life which is doomed to end in failure; the luxuriant vegetation already contains something sickly and artificially exuberant and unnatural, and turns out to be a setting for the opposite of life—death; and the death is one which Svidrigaylov himself had brought about through a violation of the girl.

SUN AND AIR

Similarly to water and vegetation, sunshine, light in general, and air are positive values, whereas darkness and lack of air are dangerous and deadening. The beauty of the cathedral flooded by sunlight ought to be felt and admired: "The cupola of the cathedral . . . glittered in the sunshine, and in the clear air every ornament on it could be plainly distinguished.". . . During the service of the dead at the Marmeladovs', an occasion which helps to stir Raskolnikov's conscience and brings him closer to the beneficent influence of Sonya, "The room was full of sunshine; the incense rose in clouds; the priest read 'Give unto her, O Lord, eternal peace'.". . . Sunshine is again associated with beauty, calm, and religion. The sun is a symbol of those forces of life which combat deadly theory.

RESURRECTION

When we turn to specifically Christian symbolism in *Crime and Punishment,* we find the outstanding images to be those of New Jerusalem, Christ's passion, and Lazarus.

The confession of Raskolnikov is described in terms reminiscent of Christ's passion on the road to Golgotha: he goes on "his sorrowful way.". . . When Raskolnikov reads in his mother's letter of Dunya's having walked up and down in her room and prayed before the Kazan Virgin, he associates her planned self-sacrifice in marrying Luzhin with the biblical prototype of self-assumed suffering for the sake of others: "Ascent to Golgotha is certainly pretty difficult". . . , he says to himself. When Raskolnikov accepts Lizaveta's cypress cross from Sonya, he shows his recognition of the significance of his taking it—the implied resolve to seek a new life though accepting suffering and punishment—by saying to Sonya, "This is the symbol of my taking up the cross.". . .

One of the central Christian myths alluded to in the novel is the story of Lazarus. It is the biblical passage dealing with Lazarus that Raskolnikov asks Sonya to read to him. The raising of Lazarus from the dead is to Dostoevsky the best *exemplum* [example] of a human being resurrected to a new life, the road to Golgotha the best expression of the dark road of sorrow, and Christ himself the grand type of voluntary suffering. "I am the Resurrection and the Life" is the refrain in this book of a man who lost his life and found it again.

The traditional emphasis of the Eastern Church is on Resurrection—of the Western, on the Passion. In *Crime and Punishment* both sides are represented: the Eastern in its promise of Raskolnikov's rebirth, the Western in the stress on his suffering. Perhaps at least part of the universality of the appeal of the novel and of its success in the West may be due to the fact that it combines the two religious tendencies.

Christian symbolism is underlined by the pagan and universal symbolism of the earth. Sonya persuades Raskolnikov not only to confess and wear the cross, but also to kiss the earth at the crossroads—a distinctly Russian and pre-Christian acknowledgment of the earth as the common mother of all men. The earth is the source of fertility and the sanction for all family and community ties. . . . In bowing to the earth and kissing it, Raskolnikov is performing a symbolic and non-rational act; the rationalist is marking the beginning of his change into a complete, organic, living human being, rejoining all other men in the community. By his crime and ideas, he had separated himself from his friends, family, and nation, in one word, he had cut himself off from Mother Earth. By the gesture of kissing the earth, he is reestablishing all his ties.

When Raskolnikov kisses the earth at the crossroads, the

meeting place of men, a bystander sarcastically suggests that
he may be saying goodby to his "children and his country"
and leaving on a pilgrimage to Jerusalem. There is deep
irony in the mocking words. Raskolnikov is indeed saying
goodby—to Petersburg, for he will be sent to Siberia. At the
same time he *is* taking farewell of his false ideal of the New
Jerusalem. In another sense, he *is* now about to embark on a
search for a new ideal, another New Jerusalem—and in this
sense he will be a pilgrim, seeking personal regeneration
which is to replace his earlier social-rationalistic ideal. Thus
at the turning point of the novel, there is a fusing of the Christian symbolism of taking up the cross and New Jerusalem
with the primeval symbolism of Gaea, Mother Earth.

THE EARTH

The epilogue [to *Crime and Punishment*] has been called unprepared for, weak, and disjointed. These strictures are natural if we pay attention exclusively to "rational" aspects of
the book and look for connections between the epilogue and
the body of the novel only in the realms of outward plot and
explicit statement. It is true that the regeneration of Raskolnikov is not presented as fully or as dramatically as the
events leading to its inception; yet its beginning and its future course are indicated sufficiently by other means. The
frequent undervaluation of the epilogue may be sympto-
matic of the lack of attention to Dostoevsky's communica-
tion through the symbolic pattern of the novel.

If we approach the epilogue with the various preparatory
strands of images clearly in our minds, what do we find?
Raskolnikov is in a Siberian city on the banks of "a broad,
deserted river," a reprise of water imagery. He has relapsed
into isolation from his fellow men; he is sunk into apathy
and gloom: "He looked at his fellow-prisoners, and was surprised at them: how they all loved life! . . . What terrible ag-
onies and tortures some of them had endured—the tramps,
for instance. Did a ray of sunshine or the primeval forest
mean so much to them? Or some cold spring in some far-
away, lonely spot which the tramp had marked three years
before and which he longed to see again as he might long to
see his mistress, dreamed of it constantly, and the green
grass around it, and the bird singing in the bush?". . . Here
. . . we see the state of the soul of the unregenerate Raskolnikov, the Lazarus before the rebirth, expressed by Dostoev-

sky through the symbolic imagery to which the novel has made us accustomed—water and vegetation. The love for life (which Raskolnikov does not yet comprehend) is represented by a spring with green grass and bushes around it.

When the regeneration of Raskolnikov begins, it is expressed in a manner still more closely linked to previously introduced imagery. His dream of the plague condemns Raskolnikov's own rationalism. It shows people obsessed by reason and will losing contact with the soil. . . . The dream is an expression of a new way of looking at reason and will—a way diametrically opposed to Raskolnikov's previous exaltation of those two faculties and rejection of all else. This dream of the plague, coming immediately before the start of the hero's regeneration, may also be another reminiscence of the Book of Revelation with its last seven plagues coming just before the millennium and the establishment of the New Jerusalem.

The epilogue then goes on to emphasize that it is the second week after Easter—the feast of Christ's passion, death, and resurrection; and that it is warm, bright spring—the season of the revival of dead nature, again a coupling of Christian and non-Christian symbolism of rebirth. . . .

The crucial final scene . . . takes place on "a bright and warm day," and "on the bank of the river.". . . The river which Raskolnikov sees now is no longer a possible means for committing suicide nor a sight inducing melancholy; it is the river of life. Calm countryside opens up before Raskolnikov across the river, where he sees nomads' tents on a steppe flooded with sunlight. They seem to be men of the age of Abraham and his flocks, truly free and living people, not living dead as Raskolnikov had been. Now he can identify himself with these nomads, although he has only one thing in common with them, the most important thing of all—humanity. A short time before, he had been cut off from his fellow-prisoners and all mankind, even those who ought to have been very close to him, his friends and family.

Then appears Sonya, and with her arrival comes the moment when Raskolnikov is suffused with love for his guide and savior. Sonya plays in the novel a part comparable to that performed by Beatrice and Lucia taken jointly in [Dante Aligheri's] *Divine Comedy.* . . . Sonya sees that all exists in God: she knows, and helps Raskolnikov to recognize, what it means to anticipate the millennium by living in rapt love for all creation here, in this world.

It was Sonya who had brought Raskolnikov the message of Lazarus and his resurrection; she had given him the cypress cross and urged him to kiss the earth at the crossroads. On the evening of the day when, by the bank of the river and in the presence of Sonya, Raskolnikov's regeneration had begun, the New Testament lies under his pillow as a reminder of the Christian prototype of resurrection which had been stressed earlier in the novel. Against the background of all the important symbols of the book, Easter, spring, Abraham's flocks, the earth of Siberia, the river, the dream, and Sonya, the drama within Raskolnikov's mind assumes its expressive outward form.

CHAPTER 3

The Idiot

The Idiot: A Success and a Failure

Elizabeth Dalton

Dostoyevsky found writing *The Idiot*, which portrays "a *positively* beautiful man," more difficult than any previous work. Though he had written about the perverse, the cruel, and the inhumane, it was in writing the story of the good Prince Myshkin that Dostoyevsky agonized most profoundly. In her book-length study of Dostoyevsky, author Elizabeth Dalton explores the peculiarities of her subject, his mental processes, and the result of the effort that produced *The Idiot.*

Dostoevsky wrote of himself in a well-known passage from his notebooks, "They call me a psychologist: this is not true. I am merely a realist in a higher sense, i.e., I depict all the depths of the human soul."

Dostoevsky was not a psychologist in the scientific, systematic way; but no great writer has ever had a more powerful understanding of the "depths," the irrational, contradictory, and perverse aspects of human life that are alien to conscious understanding. And no writer provides richer material for the study of the unconscious in literature. Indeed, Dostoevsky not only "depicts" the depths; there is in his work a sort of fascinated compulsion toward them. Each novel is a spiritual and psychological experiment with the most destructive forces in the human soul. In *The Diary of a Writer*, in a passage dealing with the Russian character, Dostoevsky speaks of "an urge for the extreme, for the fainting sensation of approaching an abyss, and half-leaning over it—to peep into the bottomless pit, and, in some very rare cases, to throw oneself into it head-forward as in a frenzy." In all of Dostoevsky's work there is this perilous flirtation with the abyss. More than any other writer, he makes cruelly seductive those aspects of experience most fraught with moral danger; and yet, in the same works, the dark forces are juxtaposed with images of great moral beauty. Out of the equivocal relationship between these opposed aspects of experience comes the extraordinary psychological excitement and aesthetic tension of Dostoevsky's fiction. Nowhere in his work are these extremes juxtaposed more dramatically than in *The Idiot*, and nowhere are the hidden connections between them so strongly suggested.

DOSTOEVSKY'S STRANGE VISION OF EXISTENCE

The Idiot is perhaps the strangest of the world's great novels. Here, even more than in Dostoevsky's other major works, one is struck with a sense of mystery, of something alien to ordinary understanding. The protagonist is one of the most attractive and lovable characters in all of literature, a good and charming young man who comes to the city to seek his fortune—like the typical protagonist of the nineteenth-century novel, the provincial outsider who conquers the sophisticated society and the desirable women of the capital. Myshkin also resembles an older figure of legend and fairy tale: the prince who comes to the rescue of the beautiful captive maiden. Yet in this case, the patterns are all strangely inverted: the prince is an epileptic, the maiden is no maiden and more than half-mad. The hero's progress through society ends not in a triumphant assertion of selfhood, but rather in a collapse of the self. And Myshkin is destroyed not by the evil designs of rivals and enemies, but paradoxically by himself and his own goodness.

At the simplest level of description, the plot of *The Idiot* might be called a love triangle, although of a very strange kind. Nastasya Filippovna, a fabulous beauty corrupted in her girlhood by an older man, is pursued by the Idiot, Prince Myshkin, who offers her Christ-like love and redemption, and by Rogozhin, a passionate and crudely powerful young merchant, who desires her with lust and hatred. Tormented by guilt and unable to accept the Prince's vision of her innocence, Nastasya vacillates between the two men and finally elopes with Rogozhin, who murders her. In the novel's last great scene, Myshkin and Rogozhin lie side by side near the dead body of Nastasya, their faces pressed together so closely that Myshkin's tears run down Rogozhin's cheeks.

The principal action of the novel is surrounded by a rich

proliferation of secondary intrigues and characters, all of them related in some degree to the primary plot. The central dynamic of the novel, however, is in the Myshkin-Nastasya-Rogozhin relationship. These three are "characters" in the usual literary sense—they are memorable and convincing personalities. But they are also, even more than Dostoevsky's other major figures, great dramatic embodiments of impulse and idea; indeed, their behavior often has less to do with the claims of the plot upon them than with the movement toward expression of the forces they embody. In the shifting patterns of action and feeling among them are represented the dynamic tensions that animate Dostoevsky's vision of existence, the contradictions between faith and reason, submission and rebellion, charity and lust. . . .

CONTRADICTIONS AND AMBIGUITIES

At the center of the novel is the extraordinary figure of the Idiot, the epileptic Prince Myshkin. The dialectic of the novel is played out around him, but within him too; in his character and his fate the other characters and their passions are included and transformed. His Christ-like will to absorb and redeem the world's hatred and evil through the total gift of himself represents the culmination of the dialectical oppositions, not in synthesis, but in transcendence of the dialectic itself. Yet this great embodiment of Dostoevsky's most powerful vision of the good is strangely flawed. Although Myshkin is moved by compassion and tenderness for everyone, the lives he touches deeply are ruined. Epileptic and apparently impotent, an "idiot" who is imposed upon by everyone, a disturbingly contradictory mixture of incapacity and saintliness, Myshkin is one of the most mysterious characters in all of literature. He is like a core of unearthly light at the center of the novel; when his personality and motives are examined they seem to dissolve in indecipherable ambiguity, a kind of negative radiance that defies analysis.

The structure of the novel itself also presents problems and ambiguities. Although *The Idiot* finally makes an effect of powerful coherence, there are obvious flaws in the progress of the narrative, gaps in the action that are never fully accounted for, unexplained comings and goings of the characters and apparently inconsistent images of their personalities, bursts of spectacular dramatic action followed by sudden lapses of tension and continuity in the narrative sequence. Mysterious holes open up in the novelistic texture, through which the entire conception threatens to disappear.

The novel occupied a crucial and troubling place in Dostoevsky's own life. He wrote to his niece Sofia Alexandrovna Ivanova:

> The idea of the novel is an old one that is dear to me, but so difficult that for a long time I didn't dare try it; if I've committed myself to it now, it's only because I was in a desperate situation. The principal idea of the novel is to portray a positively beautiful man. There is nothing more difficult in the world—especially now. All writers, not only ours, but even all the European writers, who but undertook this depiction of the *positively* beautiful man always had to give it up. Because this problem is immeasurable. The beautiful is an ideal, but the nature of that ideal—whether it be ours or that of civilized Europe—is far from having been worked out. There exists in the world only one positively beautiful person—Christ, so that the appearance of this immeasurably, infinitely beautiful person is, of course, an infinite miracle. (The whole Gospel of Saint John was conceived in this spirit; he finds the whole miracle in the one Incarnation, in the one appearance of the beautiful.) [. . .] Of the beautiful characters in Christian literature, the most fully achieved is Don Quixote; but he is beautiful simply because he is also comic. Dickens' Pickwick (an infinitely weaker conception, but nevertheless immense) is also comic, and only for that reason convinces us. Compassion is felt towards the beautiful that is mocked and does not recognize its own worth, and consequently, the readers experience sympathy. [. . .] Jean Valjean [of Hugo's *Les Misérables*] is also a powerful attempt, but he arouses sympathy through his terrible misfortune and the injustice done him by society. I have nothing similar, absolutely nothing, and that's why I'm terribly afraid it will be a failure.

The reception of *The Idiot* in Russia was somewhat disappointing, and Dostoevsky himself felt that the novel was flawed. In another letter to his niece he wrote, "I'm dissatisfied with the book, for I haven't expressed even a tenth part of what I wanted to express. Nevertheless, I don't repudiate it, and to this day I love my idea that did not succeed." And to his friend Strakhov, "In the novel much was written in haste, much is too drawn-out, much has not succeeded, but something did succeed. I am not defending the novel, but I do defend my idea."

This "idea," which was nothing less than the representation of "a positively beautiful man," a sort of Russian Christ living in the world, would continue to haunt Dostoevsky and to elude him. He tried again to deal with it in an unrealized

A SECOND-RATE NOVEL

This excerpt, from a letter written by Dostoyevsky to his publisher, shows the ambivalent feelings Dostoyevsky had about The Idiot.

I ought to tell you I have had various thoughts ticking over in my mind the entire summer and autumn (and some of them are pretty ingenious), but having to live with them has forced me to have certain misgivings about them, especially about the ones that could so easily have looked contrived, phoney or implausible. In the end I settled on a single idea, and set to work. I managed to get quite a lot down on paper, and then on the 4 December I flung everything to the devil. I can promise you that it will probably turn out a second-rate novel. But it is absolutely sickening to think that it will be second-rate and not unreservedly good.

project for a novel to be called "Atheism," and again later in a plan for a trilogy entitled "The Life of a Great Sinner," which also remained unwritten, although the plan was the source of many elements in the later works....

A NEARLY UNBEARABLE TASK

The Idiot was written during a period of intense turmoil in the author's life. Dostoevsky had gone to Europe with his new wife under threat of arrest from his creditors; he left Russia, as he wrote his friend Maikov, "to save not only my health but even my life." Epileptic seizures were occurring once a week: "it was unbearable to be fully *conscious* of the disorder of my nerves and *brain.* My reason was really falling apart,—that's the truth. I felt it; and the disorder of my nerves sometimes drove me to moments of furious madness." He went to Dresden, to Hamburg, and finally to Baden, where he and his pregnant wife installed themselves in miserable quarters above a blacksmith's forge. During these months Dostoevsky suffered an intense recurrence of his gambling mania. Every day was a dizzying succession of wins and losses; he could not leave the roulette tables until he had won brilliantly or, more often, gambled away his last farthing. At one time or another he pawned his wife's fur pelisse, her lace shawl, earrings, brooch, wedding ring, flannel petticoat, his own underdrawers. He borrowed from the novelist Goncharov, from his editor, from his wife's mother.

Finally his wife managed to get him out of Baden. They went to Geneva, where in a state of great mental agitation Dostoevsky began work on *The Idiot.*

He was to find this novel harder to write than anything he had yet done, perhaps the most difficult of all his books. For months he struggled without success to subdue and organize the material that poured into his mind. In a letter to Maikov, he wrote, "I must have worked out six plans a day (not less) on the average. My head was turned into a mill. I don't understand how I didn't lose my mind." Dostoevsky had received and spent a number of advances from his publisher, and the novel was scheduled to begin serial publication in January 1868. By December 1867 he had prepared eight different outlines without arriving at a satisfactory plan. Finally in disgust he threw out everything he had done, and after two weeks of agonizing mental effort he began writing at a furious pace an entirely "new novel," producing the first seven chapters in twenty-three days.

An Analysis of
The Idiot's
Nastasya Filippovna

Richard Curle

Dostoyevsky scholar Richard Curle uses psychological terms to help readers understand complex characters such as Nastasya Filippovna. Curle analyzes this fictional character as a flesh and blood human, citing evidence from the novel to analyze Filippovna's state of mind and character.

It is permissible to hold two diametrically opposed views about Nastasya Filippovna, the views, roughly speaking, of Prince Myshkin or of Aglaia Ivanovna, but whether we consider her as a wronged woman driven inappeasably frantic by what she has suffered or as a neurotic egoist wallowing in her misery, she remains a deeply tragic figure. For in either case she is quite unable to find harmony, and even if our pity be mitigated by the feeling that she is not really sane or our irritation heightened by her impossibly freakish conduct, yet there is always the question whether her despair is not of such a nature as to put her beyond our criticism, whether, in short, we are in a position to pass any sort of judgement upon her.

A VICTIM OF TRAGEDY

In Myshkin, who . . . is Dostoevsky's ideal self, she arouses a compassion which, turned at last into a kind of horror and darkness, is nevertheless more powerful than the bliss and sunlight brought to him by Aglaia. He sees her as both mad and doomed, the victim of an abominable outrage which has affected her mind and set her on the road to death, but he sees too that his pity and everything deriving from it can only serve to increase her wretchedness and to drive her more relentlessly to her fate:

Excerpted from Richard Curle, *Characters of Dostoevsky* (London: William Heinemann, 1950). Reprinted by permission of Random House UK Ltd.

There was something which always tortured him in the very face of this woman. Talking to Rogozhin, he had put down this sensation to his infinite pity for her, and that was the truth. That face, even in the photograph, had roused in him a perfect agony of pity: the feeling of compassion and even of suffering over this woman never left his heart, and it had not left it now. Oh no, it was stronger than ever! But Myshkin was dissatisfied with what he had said to Rogozhin; and only now at the moment of her sudden appearance he realised, perhaps through his immediate sensation, what had been lacking in his words. Words had been lacking which might have expressed horror—yes, horror. Now at this moment he felt it fully. He was certain, he was fully convinced for reasons of his own, that this woman was mad. If, loving a woman more than anything in the world, or foreseeing the possibility of loving her thus, one were suddenly to see her in chains behind an iron grating and beneath the rod of a prison warder, one would feel something like what Myshkin felt at that moment.

This extract [from Myshkin to Aglaia] summarizes, if it can be summarized—for there is a symbolic tinge in Myshkin's insight which seems, at times, to leap the barriers of normal psychology—his attitude towards this strange and unfortunate woman.

I do not believe it is possible to arrive at any final conclusion about the personality of Nastasya, for her emotional life has lost its rudder and her mingled abasement and pride ceaselessly consume her, but to get any clear idea of her at all I think one must understand, first, that her instinct is to be almost morbidly pure and that therefore, things being what they are, she must avenge herself upon herself; secondly, that she is a dreamer who has had an appalling awakening at an age when the impress of evil upon good can never be erased in a sensitive spirit; thirdly, that, as with so many self-contained people, there were forces and passions in her about which she knew nothing; and fourthly, that her brazen behaviour—how well Dostoevsky brings out the touch that, as a beautiful woman, she can do things which, as a plain woman or as a man, she would never have dared to do—is, in contrast with her real nature, a kind of desperate gesture of defiance, as if, being beyond hope or salvation, she will go to the farthest limit to deny what she cherishes.

SHAME, ANGER, AND DESTRUCTION

It would be useless, of course, to expect a logical sequence in her thoughts or acts, for not only is she more or less deranged but she is frequently swayed at one and the same mo-

ment by entirely contrary emotions; yet in general one gath-
ers a picture of her that, frightening in its intensity and bewildering in its incoherence, is nevertheless all-of-a-piece,
however blurred the details of the image. (I am inclined to
except from this her conduct at the bandstand at Pavlovsk
which has, it seems to me, a silliness and an effrontery un-
true to her special brand of extremism.) She has buried what
she valued, she has denied her youth, and, a lone wolf burning with shame and hate, she is resolved to destroy herself
in her own way. She has been tortured and she will torture;
she has been despised and she will make herself more de-
spicable still; she has lost her inward peace and therefore all
values must be cast aside.

Inherently, she is solitary and self-centred—the solitari-
ness may have been evolved from the pattern of her early
years, but the self-centredness, that potential heel of
Achilles, must have been part of her very nature—living in a
reverie like a spider at the heart of its silken web, though it
does not follow that had her life run a regular course she
would not have been capable of extreme devotion and sacrifice. She is not selfish, she is not petty, but she broods upon
her injuries with such concentrated violence that, just as
one's whole nervous system can appear to centralize on an
aching tooth, so all her experience is bound up with this
awful fact.

Let us look for a moment at her early youth. She was the
daughter of a "retired officer of good family" and, being left
an orphan at the age of seven, was brought up by a rich,
middle-aged neighbour called Totsky. By the age of twelve
she was "playful, sweet, clever and promising to become extremely beautiful" and Totsky, a typical, if shadowy, Dosto-
evskian roué, immediately laid his plans. He had her prop-
erly educated and installed in an elegant country villa
where, when she was sixteen, he appeared once more and
lived with her intermittently for four years. It was an idyllic
period according to Totsky's reckoning, whose annual visits
lasted but a few months, but how little he guessed what was
going on in her brain! The meek and yielding Nastasya was
maturing in secret and when she discovered that he was
planning to marry an heiress, a very different Nastasya was
revealed, a mocking, vindictive Nastasya who frightened
him to such a degree that he had to shelve the idea of marriage and, instead, provide the girl he had been about to

abandon with an apartment in Petersburg. Another five years passed, five uneasy years for Totsky, and then, resolved at the age of fifty to free himself at last and marry, he sought to buy her off with a gift of seventy-five thousand roubles and to espouse her to a man who, quite obviously, was only after the money. It is at this stage that we meet her.

A BLEAK VIEW BEGETS TRAGIC RESULTS

I have given this brief summary because ... I think that many readers of *The Idiot* slur over these pages—she has not yet appeared on the scene to arouse our interest—and thus miss perhaps the one glimpse which might reveal the latent woman who was warped and changed by her discovery that life was rotten at the core and that she had been caught up in its rottenness. It was this other woman who, like some envenomed, lovely flower emerged from its bud, had so alarmed Totsky, but though she despised and detested him, it was primarily against herself that she had rebelled. It was not only the injury, it was the insult; the ruin not alone of her body but of her being. Henceforward nothing counted, and if Totsky was thrown contemptuously aside like an old shoe, the thing he represented spelt destruction.

Something in her had slowly gathered force, and the simplicity of her character, as shown even in Petersburg by her friendship for simple people while living under Totsky's protection, had yielded to that complex and incalculable other self which had its hidden roots in despair and madness. Such was the woman who, in her triumphant beauty, had enslaved Rogozhin and stricken Myshkin's heart. But did Rogozhin want to understand her and did Myshkin attempt to approach her through her atrophied simplicity?

Nastasya Filippovna is an enigma, and it is probable that Dostoevsky meant her to be an enigma. But, as I said before, she is none the less a tragic figure. Her tragedy is, in part, a tragedy of temperament. True, she has suffered great wrongs, for if she appears to have been amenable to Totsky at first, one may regard that attitude either as a sort of numbness gathering hate in silence or as a recognition that, if all be lost, nothing matters; but her experience, however horrible, would not have been too harrowing for the recovery of her mental balance had she been other than what she was. But there is a feverishness about her nature, a seething depth of sickly introspection, which will allow neither for forgetfulness nor for forgiveness. She is enveloped in sin and desecration and the very outline of her personality has altered beyond recognition.

SOME QUESTIONS THAT REMAIN UNANSWERED

It is perhaps a mere coincidence that just as her personality eludes us, so her physical presence eludes us. We cannot see her clearly, and though Myshkin reads much into her photograph—he has not met her yet—what he reads does not bring her really before us:

> The portrait was indeed of a wonderfully beautiful woman. She had been photographed in a black silk dress of an extremely simple and elegant cut; her hair, which looked as though it were dark brown, was arranged in a simple homely style; her eyes were dark and deep, her brow was pensive; her expression was passionate and, as it were, disdainful. She was rather thin in the face and perhaps pale.

Deep sadness was depicted there no doubt, but words cannot describe the inner quality of expression or of bearing, and it is clear that there was something in her face and presence that gave to her beauty a significance which could attract irresistibly such diverse types as Myshkin and Rogozhin.

What then was it about her that, quite apart from the deliberate wildness of her behaviour, made her stand out from the crowd? Was the urge that drove her on the ultimate expression of an extraordinary, hard-pressed personality or was she the slave of a powerful, wounded egocentricity which, by reason of her looks, she could impose on men? Or again, was she a pathological type, unstable from the beginning and now beyond all psychological disentanglement?

Such questions cannot be answered with any authority, but I feel that we must keep before us that picture of her youth and realize that her innocence, even when lost, conventionally speaking, was still part of her—for innocence, in one interpretation, is a state of mind—though she believed it had gone for ever. We know little of that terrible month she spent with Myshkin, but it is evident from his scattered and reluctant words that the most agonizing times were those in which she sought, with frenzy, to exculpate herself and to declare that she was guiltless. As Myshkin says to Aglaia:

> Oh, she's crying out every minute in her frenzy that she doesn't admit going wrong, that she was the victim of others, the victim of a depraved and wicked man. But whatever she may say to you, believe me, she's the first to disbelieve it, and

to believe with her whole conscience that she is . . . to blame. When I tried to dispel that gloomy delusion, it threw her into such misery that my heart will always ache when I remember that awful time. It's as though my heart had been stabbed once for all. She ran away from me. Do you know what for? Simply to show me that she was a degraded creature. But the most awful thing is that perhaps she didn't even know herself that she only wanted to prove that to me, but ran away because she had an irresistible inner craving to do something shameful, so as to say to herself at once, "There, you've done something shameful again, so you're a degraded creature!"

These outbursts, as Myshkin discerned, are themselves an inverted confession of guilt—that is to say, of guilt as she conceived of it—seeking in vain for an anodyne, and never does she really visualize any hope for herself. But why, one asks again and again, did she ever allow herself to become Totsky's mistress or, at least, not struggle to free herself from an intolerable position? Of course, as I suggested before, there are natures which, appearing to surrender what they value most, are inwardly planning revenge—as she said to him later, she "had never had any feeling in her heart for him except contempt—contempt and loathing which had come upon her after her first surprise"—but though her own explanation to Myshkin is that she was frightened of killing herself, is it not more probable that this is no more than a half-truth, as so many rationalized explanations of obscure emotions are, and that, once she had recovered from the initial shock, a deeper instinct was to taste the very dregs of degradation in order that her punishment might be one long agony of loathing and remorse? Even when, in her recklessness, she promises to marry Rogozhin, she tells him "there's nothing but ruin anyway"—one of the most revealing remarks she makes in the whole book—and, as we know, she foresaw that marriage with him would be her death warrant.

Her relations with this turbulent man have a significance beyond the personal. She feels contempt for him, but she also feels that kind of respect—only that is not quite the right word—which comes from the knowledge that, until he kills her, he will do anything for her; but what she feels in the main—I say "in the main", for there is also the idea that by marrying him she will save Myshkin from marrying her—is that he is her nemesis and, as one might put it, the blind instrument of her fate. She fears him, but she does not shrink from him; in fact, she is drawn back to him whenever she tries to escape. For she knows that there is no new life for her and that Rogozhin is the high priest of the sacrificial offering.

All the same, she struggles against her destiny because, with the advent of Myshkin, something which she believed to be dead wakens again in her. She had met him only a few hours when she said to him:

> I used to think and dream, think and dream, and I was always imagining someone like you, kind, good and honest, and so stupid that he would come forward all of a sudden and say "You are not to blame, Nastasya Filippovna, and I adore you." I used to dream like that, till I nearly went out of my mind.... And then this man would come, stay two months in a year, bringing shame, corruption, degradation, and go away.

As she gets to know Myshkin better, this first impression, deepening from day to day, masters her as completely as, in her insane and incessant brooding, anything could master her. But her pride, which is that of the damned who condemn themselves but will not hear a word, whether of blame or pity, from others, is, in its own way, as dominant as her abasement, and her perception that Myshkin's feeling for her, however profound, is only compassion drives her more frantic than ever. This pride of hers, the pride which had made her treat Rogozhin, her future murderer, as a lackey, this pitiable refuge to which she had clung, had received a mortal blow, and though in the ghastly scene with Aglaia towards the close of the book—among the most painful things in Dostoevsky—she is able to hold her own against the infuriated girl's blistering attack, yet the knowledge that it was she, Aglaia, whom Myshkin loved and that she was entitled to throw it in her face was for her the end of everything despite her Pyrrhic victory. And perhaps, indeed, the truth of Aglaia's words, distorted though they were by jealousy on the one hand and by indignation on Myshkin's account on the other, found a reverberating echo in her own heart. Yes, such an echo, ruinous in its implications, may well have flashed through her when listening to Aglaia's implacable denunciation:

> I felt sorry for Prince Lyov Nikolayevitch from the day when I first made his acquaintance, and heard afterwards what happened at your party. I felt sorry for him, because he is such a simple-hearted man and in his simplicity believed that he might be happy ... with a woman ... of such a character. What I was afraid of for him came to pass. You were inca-

pable of loving him, you tortured him and abandoned him. You could not love him, because you were too proud . . . no, not proud, that's a mistake, but too vain . . . that's not it either, it's your self-love which amounts almost to madness, of which your letters to me are a proof. You couldn't love a simple-hearted man like him, and very likely you secretly despised and laughed at him. You can love nothing but your shame and the continued thought that you've been brought to shame and humiliation.

Could it be true that, in its special form, self-love *had* been her undoing from first to last, was even her surrender to Totsky as masochistic in its origin as her imminent surrender to Rogozhin? Did such thoughts perchance come to her then in the emptiness of her triumph?

There follows for Nastasya and Myshkin a sort of lull, a sort of oblivious peace, in which she tastes a spurious felicity, but in reality it was all over. Too soon the trance was shattered and she was driven, hysterical but open-eyed, into the murderous arms of Rogozhin. She knew that death awaited her, but she had reached a pitch of nihilistic desperation where it was the only release and the only solution.

Sources of Inspiration for *The Idiot*'s Nastasya Filippovna

Jacques Catteau

Jacques Catteau is a professor of Russian language and literature at the University of Paris Sorbonne. In the following essay, Catteau shows how Dostoyevsky's own reading influenced the plot, theme, and characters of *The Idiot*. Part media event, part history, part previous literary character, Nastasya Filippovna was created slowly. Early drafts of *The Idiot* reveal three distinct sources of inspiration: First was the character Mignon, created by German writer Johann Wolfgang von Goethe, whose work Dostoyevsky knew intimately. The second was Egyptian queen Cleopatra as described by fellow Russian writer Aleksandr Pushkin. The third source of inspiration was the true story of Olga Umetskaya, a severely abused fifteen-year-old girl who had attempted, more than once, to burn down her family's home.

> Every newspaper is nothing but a tissue of horrors from first line to last. War, crimes, thefts, lewdness, tortures, crimes of princes, crimes of nations, crimes of individuals, intoxication with universal atrocity. And every civilised man drinks this disgusting brew with his morning meal. Everything in this world reeks of crime: the newspaper, the wall, the face of man.
> I cannot understand how a pure hand can touch a newspaper without a shudder of disgust.
>
> Charles Baudelaire, Mon coeur mis à nu

Unlike Baudelaire, who was writing in the 1860s, Dostoyevsky considered the Press an indispensable tool with nothing sordid about it. In this field he was the initiator of the great American and European literatures of the twentieth century,

Excerpted from Jacques Catteau, *Dostoyevsky and the Process of Literary Creation*, translated by Audrey Littlewood. Copyright ©1989 by Cambridge University Press. Reprinted by permission of Cambridge University Press.

where the newspaper, even in its raw form, is an integral part of the novel.

Dostoyevsky could not live without the Press, especially abroad, where he needed to keep in touch with his native country. In Geneva, in 1867 and 1868, he found true 'happiness' in reading the Russian Press from cover to cover: *The Voice, The Moscow Bulletin, The St Petersburg Bulletin,* and the foreign papers. He is always mentioning his newspaper reading in his letters. And the two hours, from five to seven, which he spent on this daily activity in some café, were so enthralling to him that, while he was walking in the evening with his young wife, he loved to tell her what he had been reading about, so that she could keep up with 'everything that was happening in Russia'.

News Items in Creative Research

Once he was so indignant about a story that Anna Grigoryevna noted the event in her *Diary* of 14 October 1867 (2 October of the Russian calendar). 'In the evening we went for a walk and Fedya told me a long story of what he had been reading in the papers, that is the story of Olga Umetskaya, poor girl; how sorry I felt, what strength of character.' The story filled the Russian legal chronicle and Dostoyevsky followed the trial attentively in the Russian newspapers he found in Geneva. . . . Dostoyevsky's strong reaction is understandable: he might have created Olga Umetskaya himself. At fifteen, she was still a child but already a woman, and desperation had driven her to rebel.

The Umetskys, well-off provincial landowners but always squabbling about money, were what would now be called inadequate parents. Carefree progenitors, they would leave their children in a village in the heart of the steppes until they were seven or eight. Then they took them into the family, but it was a martyrdom for the survivors (five out of twenty), who were regularly beaten and sent to sleep in the stable, so that the two little brothers of Olga 'did not know how to speak' at seven years old. Olga had twice tried to throw herself out of the window, and even to hang herself, but each time she had been stopped. Finally, in desperation, she tried to burn the family house down four times: just before the last attempt she had been beaten black and blue for giving some honey to a workman. Brought to court, this humiliated and injured soul was proud enough to take complete responsibility for her action and to deny nothing.

The future creator of Nastasya Filippovna understood her perfectly, and was much struck by the picture of this family of Russian provincial nobility, rent by money quarrels and gnawed by the leprosy of dirt and disorder. He had been working on a similar theme for about a month: life was strewing manna in his path.

The first sketch of the novel *The Idiot,* on 14 September 1867, begins with the words: 'A family of ruined landowners.' Certainly the situation is different; the characters have a 'name' and live in Petersburg. The father is a general who was ruined abroad and is trying 'to get money by stupid calculations'. The mother is 'worthy of respect, noble but extravagant'. There is not much resemblance to the Umetskys: the son, 'the handsome young man' is proud and ambitious 'with some claim to originality' (the future Ganya): the daughter is 'stupid, cruel and bourgeois', the second son, nicknamed 'the Idiot' because he is epileptic and his mother hates him, is a soul who has 'a burning need for love and immeasurable pride' (a very distant predecessor of Myshkin). But there is also an adopted child, an orphan (daughter of the mother's sister-in-law): 'a resentful Mignon and Cleopatra'. The poor orphan is terribly ill-treated and 'less than a servant in the house'. 'Naive, proud, envious' she hates the family and longs for revenge; she is also 'terribly intelligent and notices everything'. She tells her dreams to the Idiot, with whom she forms an alliance, since they are both humiliated. Like the future Nastasya Filippovna, she has been physically humiliated; the general tries to rape her; the 'handsome young man', 'the Idiot' and in later plans a certain Vladimir manage to do so.

She is 'the resentful Mignon and Cleopatra' at the same time. Dostoyevsky was creating his heroine with reference to his cultural heritage, thus beginning his dialogue with 'great literature'. Mignon is the heroine of *Wilhelm Meisters Lehrjahre,* by [German writer Johann Wolfgang von] Goethe, a strange child uprooted from her family, who accompanies a *troupe* of wandering actors, singing nostalgic airs from the country 'where the lemon trees bloom' and finally dies of love for Wilhelm. Dostoyevsky transforms this image to represent the bitter poetry of loneliness and the deadly power of dreams of love. Cleopatra, as we have seen, is a disturbing and powerful beauty with the soul of a praying mantis, a legacy from Russian poet, Aleksandr Pushkin's *Egyptian Nights*. She is more than an image of debauchery; Dostoyevsky was fascinated by her 'ferocious irony', her desire to 'enjoy the contempt' which she feels towards the suitors for the deadly night of love, or in other words, her pleasure in vengeance. Like Cleopatra, his heroine dreams of revenge on those who possess or rape her. And like the queen, who, for one night, wishes to become a low courtesan, a slave, she proposes, in an extreme challenge, to become 'a bad woman'.

This was the first sketch. And suddenly reality, in the form of a news item, had given a seal of authenticity to the literary figure which he was drawing with the help of images from Goethe and Pushkin. Dostoyevsky took up his notebook at page 27 and opposite 'resentful Mignon' he wrote in the margin 'Olga Umetskaya'. On page 29 he added directly: 'The story of Mignon is just the same as the story of Olga Umetskaya.' Reality, enhanced by the sanction of public opinion since it was a fact chosen by the press as an example of a social tendency, fertilised the research which had begun with the cultural background and personal inspiration of the writer. It was still a long way to the complex living figure of Nastasya Filippovna, the result of trial and error, hesitation and changes, as well as many experiments with successive heroines: Mignon, Hero, the very real Olga Umetskaya, the newcomers Ustinya and Nastya. But Dostoyevsky now knew that he was going forward on a path cleared by reality, and that the tragic figure, extravagant as it might seem, was not an arbitrary construction, but a creature living in this world. Reality freed the artist from the poet's doubts. In fact, this operation remained hidden; the contemporary reader of Dostoyevsky, unlike the critic who has access to the notebooks, was aware only of the fascinating Nastasya Filippovna, though he sensed some truth behind the image. Dostoyevsky, with the science of the true realist, had used the vague and dark background of buried but still palpable memories of things read before. This was not a simple procedure, but a characteristic of the way in which Dostoyevsky constructed the novel: he did not describe reality or give it a concrete image, but allowed its presence to be felt, and admitted its first existence. Reality was thus no longer the projection, the transcribed perception of the author, but emerged from the heroes, as it was an essential part of them when they were first created.

CHAPTER 4

Notes from the Underground

READINGS ON

FYODOR DOSTOYEVSKY

Notes from the Underground Presents a Romanticized View of Freedom

Malcolm V. Jones

British scholar and lecturer Malcolm V. Jones has written numerous articles on nineteenth-century Russian literature. His major study of Dostoyevsky, from which this essay is excerpted, focuses on six of Dostoyevsky's better-known works. In this selection, Jones uses psychological and philosophical methods to illuminate the complex nature of Dostoyevsky's unnamed anti-hero in *Notes from the Underground*, a character commonly referred to by critics and readers as the Underground Man. By placing the intensely felt passions of the Underground Man up against the pragmatism of the man's peers, Jones reveals how Dostoyevsky is able to illustrate the limitations of idealist thought whether it be "Romantic," like that of the Underground Man, or "Rational," as was the fashion among many intellectuals of Dostoyevsky's time.

It may well be, as is often said, that the most important problem posed in *Notes from Underground* is the problem of freedom. If one reads the book as a psychological document, this is a very probable conclusion. If one regards it, in [critic] Walter Kaufmann's words, as "the best overture for existentialism ever written," there is no getting away from a similar verdict. Even if one takes it as a contribution to the ideological polemics of Dostoyevsky's own day, as a vibrant protest against rationalist, utilitarian, and determinist philosophies, as Joseph Frank does [in his study of *Notes from Underground*], it is still the problem of freedom which comes to the fore.

From Malcolm V. Jones, *Dostoyevsky: The Novel of Discord* (London: Paul Elek, 1976). Copyright ©1976 by Malcolm V. Jones. Reprinted by permission of the author.

But this does not mean that it is necessarily most helpful to begin one's analysis at this point; nor does it mean that it is necessarily the fundamental problem. More fundamental would be the question *why* the Underground Man is obsessed by freedom; and not only freedom, but self-respect, the laws of nature, malice and perversity. Indeed the Underground Man presents his reader with a whole series of rhetorical questions (which he answers himself—indeed this is his whole point in asking them). All of them amount to one central thing: why do I behave in such a perverse, inappropriate, unseemly, unattractive, immoral, anti-social way? We, his readers, are presumed to be too normal, respectable and well-adjusted to understand this. Many readers actually seem to get so caught up in the Underground Man's predicament that they forget their own supposed identity in the fiction. But this is important. It sets the tone of that normality against which the Underground Man persistently offends.

The first part of *Notes from Underground* is the better known and is occasionally published on its own in the West. Freedom as a philosophical concept is a central theme in it. What is of fundamental importance is the Underground Man's exceptional consciousness of the irreducible complexity of life and his inability to cope with it or engage in consistent and worthwhile action. His sense of impotence, alienation, resentment, self-humiliation should be understood in terms of this primary problem, an inability to find any bearings in life which are adequate to life's complexity, to make ideal and reality connect, to discover in himself an effective Idea.

Almost at the end of his notes, the Underground Man observes:

> We do not even know where living reality is, what it is, nor what it is called. Leave us alone without our books and we immediately grow confused and lose our way. We don't know what to adhere to nor what to follow, what to love, what to hate, what to respect or what to despise. We even grow weary of being human beings—human beings with their *own*, real flesh and blood.

This is the beginning and the end of the Underground Man's problems. Life is too complex, man is too complex; man has lost his way, his sense of values, his sense of perspective; he has no firm base on which to stand and from which to launch into spontaneous and resolute action; he suffers from a chronic lack of self-confidence, oversensitivity and an acute identity-crisis; he cannot be sure even of his own motives—unless, that is, he is able to close his eyes to the spiritual problems of his age, to take refuge in the simplistic solutions of progressive ideologies, or is just too stupid to notice. As Dostoyevsky wrote many years later: 'The underground is caused by the destruction of belief in general principles. "There is nothing holy."'

A PAINFUL BACKGROUND

Dostoyevsky chose the form of the confession for his work (its original title was *Ispoved'*, A Confession), which enabled him to depict perfectly not only the disorder, but also the peculiar kind of emotionally based logic which underlies the Underground Man's discourse—the digressions, the apparent irrelevances, the intentionally inappropriate and tasteless remarks, and the unseemly tone. To understand why the hero's discourse develops as it does, one has to understand not only the ideological polemic, but also the hero's psychological problems and background. None of this is a mystery. The Man from Underground asks for nothing better than the opportunity to display his psychological disorder in public——or, at least, to play at it. The psychological background, as distinct from the actuality, is provided mostly in Part Two, where the hero recalls episodes from his past, illustrative of his insuperable problems in achieving social integration.

At the age of twenty-four, the Underground Man is as solitary as a savage. He has no friends or intimates. His colleagues regard him as an eccentric and find him embarrassing and distasteful. He possesses boundless vanity, but loathes himself. He tries to look distinguished and refined, but succeeds only in affecting a loutish expression. Like many a hero of a nineteenth-century novel, he had been left an orphan as a small boy and was cowed by constant scolding. He grew up prematurely silent, introspective and exceptionally sensitive. His schoolmates had jeered at him because he was different from them. This he could not stand and he shut himself up in a world of nervous, sensitive, boundless pride. They jeered at his ungainly figure and unprepossessing face, while he marvelled at their stupidity and limited horizons. He yearned for real comrades, but his relationships always turned out to be unnatural and unequal.

So here is the background to the Underground Man's neurosis. The description of a deprived childhood, of the lot of the orphan, was already, of course, a commonplace in European and Russian literature; so, in Russian literature, was the lot of the poor civil service clerk. But, as usual in the works of his maturity, Dostoyevsky transcends convention. The Underground Man displays a sense of not belonging, of alienation from others, of being inadequate for their company; but at the same time a sense of being superior in intellect and sensibility. These attitudes are nurtured in him by his exclusion from the company of his comrades and his inability to mix with them, and also—significantly—by his immersion in Romantic literature. He cannot assert himself according to their unreflective values, which he despises; if he asserts himself according to his own idealistic lights, he is misunderstood, ridiculed and banished from society. Participation in life appears impossible to him, yet he yearns for it. The only behaviour patterns which he is able or willing to adopt in company are totally inappropriate to his goal of social integration. The more this is borne in on him, the more exaggeratedly inappropriate his response.

LOFTY NOTIONS LEAD TO FAILURE

He introduces himself at the beginning of Part Two as a 'typical educated man of the nineteenth century' with advanced tendencies. He is refined, but a moral coward and a slave. He is afraid of life and tries to withdraw from it into anonymous routine, but this does not save him from his inner conflict, which demands an outlet and a resolution. There is nothing in daily life which attracts him and which he can respect, so he finds consolation in reading. [Dostoyevsky scholar] Richard Peace has rightly reminded us that fiction is a key concept in the work. 'The underground man finds it impossible to distinguish between fact and fiction,' largely, it may be added, because fiction supplies him with the values which are missing in real life. He is a living example of Dostoyevsky's fear that if man departs from the structures of reality, art will depart with him.

The Man from Underground is not, therefore, without ideas and ideals. . . . But [they offer] him no permanent sanctuary, for, as he argues, Russian Romanticism is not like German and French transcendental romanticising: Russian Romantics comprehend everything, see everything, and often see everything incomparably more clearly than more practical minds do. They cherish within themselves 'the sublime and the beautiful' but they are also rogues. Their 'many-sidedness' is amazing and they combine within themselves the most opposite of qualities. Hence, according to the Underground Man, the Russian Romantic's chronic vacillation and indecision. Of course, books can soothe him, stimulate him, cause him pain, and drown in a flood of impressions the disorder seething within him, but he tires of them and yearns for reality again. Despairing of reconciling his ideal with reality he plunges into vice and debauchery, and then plunges back again into convulsions of weeping and hysteria. His dreams of the 'sublime and the beautiful' come with greater strength after a bout of dissipation. Sometimes he yields to a sort of blind belief that one day, by some miracle, present reality will burst its fetters and before him will stretch a horizon of productive, congenial and rewarding activity, and that he will ride into the world crowned with laurels. Sometimes, after such dreaming, he feels impelled to embrace humanity in general. This obliges him to go forth and seek out at least one concrete human being who soon disabuses him of his dreams and strips him of his illusions.

There is no need to tax the patience of the reader by recalling the anecdotes told by the Underground Man in illustration of his past life. He engages in what becomes almost a cult of inappropriate behaviour. The goal of social integration is inconsistent with his lofty ideals and also with his need to dominate others. His resentment, depravity and malice are inconsistent with his fine words and dreams. He feels socially humiliated and morally degraded. He becomes hyperconscious of elements of deceit and incongruity in himself. Finally he rejects the possibility of regeneration through the pure prostitute Liza—in part another projection of his Romantic ideals—because he does not believe in the purity of his own motives. The failure of reality to match up to the hero's ideals draws forth in him sado-masochistic tendencies from which he can find no escape and which he comes to enjoy. . . .

A ROMANTIC IN THE AGE OF REASON

What Dostoyevsky shows in Part One is how these emotional problems interact with the new cultural situation which arose in Russia in the 1860s, a period in which scientific determinism, rational self-interest, utilitarianism, the anthropological principle, became fashionable among advanced intellectuals. In 1864 the arguments of Part One were of topical interest to his informed readers; hence its dominant position in the work. But chronologically it comes second and it requires some such explanation as that furnished in the second part. The reader needs to understand with whom he is dealing and who is dealing with him. In brief, the picture with which Part Two presents us is of an individual whose inability to cope with the complexity of life and his own nature (in particular an artificially stimulated idealism) has given rise to uncontrollable conflicts in his personality, to resentment, to a desire to humiliate and be humiliated. His future preoccupation with freedom is implicit in his story: he is constantly talking of slavery and his desire for mastery. But his sense of impotence in confronting the world and in controlling his own inner conflicts is everywhere made manifest. He is unable to exert his willpower effectively. He feels eminently unfree. He can assert himself only in perversity and rancour, which bring their own retribution.

So what can the progressive intellectuals of the 1860s do for him, or to him? With these too he is acquainted only through the printed word, which in matters of philosophy as in the realms of fiction exercises a tremendous power over his imagination.

In Part One the Underground Man is already forty, but he has not lost his Romantic attitudes. He believes that hypersensitivity is both a mark of superiority and a curse. He sees himself as an outcast, who must withdraw from society. His rejection of mathematical models of reality is part of the very life-blood of Romanticism, as is also his tendency to assert or assume that the nature of his own personality must be a truer reflection of ultimate reality than any 'scientific law'. So too is his cult of passion and irrationalism: the revolt against Reason.

It is not difficult to see why a man obsessed by his own impotence might fall prey to the scientific determinism of the 1860s, to the idea that man is but a piano key—views which seem to confirm his worst suspicions about his own powerlessness. If true, they also—and this is a different but equally important consequence—absolve him from moral responsibility for his own degradation, over which he feels he has no ultimate control.

It is also not difficult to see why he cannot accept the supposed rationality of life and man's supposed capacity to act rationally once he has perceived his own interests. He discovers within himself every day elements of the most contradictory order conceivable. But these reactions do not solve his problems; they compound them.

By the time he is forty, the Underground Man has plunged deeper into the mire; he no longer tries to overcome his weakness, but actually experiences a strange pleasure in the feeling that there is no escape from his degradation, because the fundamental scientifically accredited laws of nature decree that he can never become a new man.

Just as formerly he had yearned to be thrown out of the pub, so now he yearns to be struck a blow in the face, for the sheer pleasure of feeling desperate and knowing there is nothing that can be done about it. Whereas before he had taken two years to wreak his elaborate and petty revenge on the officer, now he knows that he can never really revenge himself, because he can never make up his mind to a course of action.

A SIMPLISTIC THEORY IS REJECTED

Now, however, he is not merely a victim of a neurosis. He can offer an explanation of his situation in accordance with the laws of scientific determinism. As [critic] Joseph Frank says:

> The tragedy of the underground man does not arise, as is popularly supposed, because of his rejection of reason. It derives from his acceptance of *all* the implications of 'reason' in its then-current Russian incarnation—and particularly those implications which the advocates of reason . . . preferred to overlook or deny.

Though this passage tells only a part of the truth, it is an important part which is often overlooked.

His alienation from his philistine comrades is formalised as the difference between the Man of Action or the Man of Nature and the man of acute sensibility, who realises how ineffectual he is by comparison. If he receives an insult, he harbours the desire for revenge, and surrounds it with a quagmire of doubts, reasonings, questionings, misunderstandings. There is nothing for him to do but retire into his stinking mousehole with a deprecatory smile, and immerse himself in malicious rancour. This poison of unsatisfied wishes penetrates inwards. The mouse does not really know whether he is powerless or not. That is what underlies the strange pleasure of which the Underground Man speaks.

But although a sense of impotence dominates him, the Man from Underground ultimately refuses to accept it. He declares that he will not accept anything, any so-called impossibility. He will not accept that twice two makes four, or the limitations placed upon him by the 'laws of Nature'. One must even accept that one is to blame for everything, even though it may appear that one is completely innocent.

All his life he has engaged in posturing and play-acting and acts of provocation to escape from the ennui, the boredom, that follows from a feeling of impotence. He takes revenge simply from spite. He attacks those philosophers who argue that if man could perceive his rational interests he would cease to do nasty things and immediately become noble and good. History is full of people who, knowing their own interests, have deliberately opted for the wilful and the eccentric, the unseemly and the perverse. Systems and logical arguments fly in the face of reality. Civilisation has not made man less aggressive; it has merely made him more complex and increased the variety of his appetites and sensations.

Notes from the Underground Presents an Argument Against Radicalism

Louis Breger

Louis Breger's experience as a psychoanalyst helped provide the structure for his fifth book, a study of Dostoyevsky's life and writing. Drawing on letters and diaries as well as fiction, Breger looks at the people and circumstances that influenced the great author. The following selection focuses on a particular irritant in Dostoyevsky's life, a young radical named Nikolay G. Chernyshevsky. In the early 1860s, shortly after the publication of Chernyshevsky's political novel *What Is to Be Done?*, Dostoyevsky's notebooks were filled with arguments against Chernyshevsky's philosophy, sometimes known as rationalism for its absolute faith in science and reason. Rationalism bothered Dostoyevsky in part because of a certain strident, self-satisfied tone employed by many of Chernyshevsky's followers. Too independent to simply side with more conservative forces, Dostoyevsky began forming his own argument against the rationalism of his time. This argument became a guiding force behind *Notes from the Underground*.

In the early 1860s, debate over a wide range of social, moral, and political questions was carried on in journals that espoused different points of view.... Dostoevsky ... stood somewhere between the [conservatives] and the radicals.

[Nikolay G.] Chernyshevsky, the best known of the radicals, blended French utopian socialism and English utilitarianism into a vision of a future world of love and moral perfection. His philosophy, as expounded in articles and the extremely popular novel *What Is to Be Done?* (published in 1863), presented a version of ideas current in Europe at the time. He espoused the "unity of nature," the belief that man has no special nature, that free will is an illusion, and that a common set of scientific laws govern rocks, trees, and people. There is a great faith in science and reason in all this, a widespread nineteenth century phenomenon, a faith that remains very much alive today. Chernyshevsky assumes that there are laws of human life, of the same form as the laws of physical science and, if we have not discovered them yet, we soon will and can govern ourselves accordingly. This general faith in science and reason was taken to mean that all human conduct is—or could be—directed by rational self-interest. People do what is necessary for self-preservation—there is no inherent good or evil—and, since they are presumed to be rational, education will lead to a society that runs smoothly along planned lines; everyone will live harmoniously, satisfying themselves and helping others. A related aspect of this set of beliefs was materialism. A concern to better the material lot of the vast understratum of Russian society was taken to an extreme; man was seen as entirely a creature of material needs; satisfy these and you eliminate human problems and conflicts. . . . [T]his [philosophy] took an antiart form, and various examples were given of how farmers and workers contributed more than artists and writers.

FICTION PROVIDES A LASTING ARGUMENT

Dostoevsky thought all this was nonsense; his observations of society and human life, and his insight into himself, had led to a very different—a much more complex—view of man. He was inflamed by the certainty and self-satisfied tone of the radicals and discerned the hostility beneath their professed desire to help others and perfect society. Chernyshevsky's views . . . offended his deepest personal sympathies. He was nothing if not an individualist, and his novels—both before and after this period—are filled with characters who struggle to assert their uniqueness. He was also a man who lived in his imagination; the center of his existence, from adolescence on, was built on literature and an identification with great writers. In the creation of literature he expressed his individuality and revealed truths about human nature that had only partly to do with "reason"—they came more from imagination, dream, and emotion. Man's urge for freedom was as important as—and often more important than—his material needs; literature should never be conscripted to serve political ends. . . . His private *Notebooks* are filled with scoffing references to the utilitarian ideas of the radicals of which the following is typical: "[the radicals strive] to prove that there is nothing beyond what the belly contains. Let them dare to deny it. They admit *with pride:* boots are better than Shakespeare." He was also very antagonistic to what he saw as their attempt to force life into theory; there are many references to Chernyshevsky's ignorance of real life.

Dostoevsky's sensitivity to hostility made him very aware of its presence, in thin disguise, within the radical's rhetoric. One of his strongest convictions was that we need beliefs and ideals to counter our anger and selfishness. A good deal of his journalism was devoted to the search for unity and reconciliation—between radicals and conservatives, Slavophiles and westernizers—and his own quest for Christian belief—never a certainty with him, always a search—was the principal area in which he sought a unifying ideal. The radicals believed that if restraints were removed and people allowed to pursue self-interest, a reasonable and harmonious system would evolve. Dostoevsky felt, and attempted to demonstrate in his novels, that this would simply give license to the most amoral, self-willed destructiveness. This brings us to the consideration of how his arguments were transformed into fiction.

The opening monologue of *Notes from Underground* contains a fairly direct satire of Chernyshevsky's views. Dostoevsky shows how a reasonable, "perfected" society would be an intolerable constraint on one's freedom. Confronted with such a society, his protagonist chooses to assert his individuality in whatever way he can. But the novelist demonstrates this—and here is the crucial point—not with argument or a political tract like *What Is to Be Done?* but by creating a great literary character—the Underground Man—who takes on a life of his own. As this happens, the novel moves into realms far beyond the argument with Chernyshevsky, realms that are more personal and, at the same time, of broader significance.

CHAPTER 5

The Brothers Karamazov

The Brothers Karamazov: A Different Kind of Morality Tale

Peter Conradi

Full of violence, scandal, and perversion, *The Brothers Karamazov* yet remains a novel of faith and beauty. Peter Conradi, author of *Fyodor Dostoevsky*, a book-length study of the writer and his works, shows that only by vividly portraying the most blasphemous and disgraceful people does Dostoyevsky leave the reader no doubt as to the harrowing results of evil. By combining deeply troubling details of his own life with folktale-like elements, Dostoyevsky created his own enduring fable. It remains one of the most complex studies of good and evil ever attempted.

Dostoevsky's last novel is also his greatest, and among the greatest of all novels. Its moral passion has a sublime grandeur, its story a sensational, stark beauty. A passionate simplicity marks its delineation of character, while its themes—religious faith and doubt, love and rebellion, disintegration and renewal, and, above all, the terrible mysteries of good and evil—are intricately 'worked'. It is a novel about the murder of a father by his own child (parricide), and a massive false trail leads the reader to believe, against his will, that Mitya must have perpetrated this act. We read, therefore, for suspense at the level of story, as well as for metaphysical suspense at the level of idea-play. The centre of this idea-play (atheism) and the subject of the story (parricide), moreover, echo each other: each concerns the overthrow of the father, earthly or heavenly, the rejection of authority, human and divine. [While he was imprisoned] in Siberia Dostoevsky had been much struck by Ilyinsky, a convict falsely convicted for parricide. His own father's [mysterious] death [while he was away at school] may have left him

From *Fyodor Dostoevsky* by Peter Conradi. Copyright © Peter Conradi. Reprinted with permission of St. Martin's Press, Inc.

with an unquiet conscience: his father's estate contained the village of Chermashnya, which figures on the Karamazov estate and is associated by both Ivan and Mitya with their guilt.

A CONCENTRATED VISION

The story builds the clarity of a folk-tale into a complex picture, as Dostoevsky intended, of contemporary educated Russia. There are three brothers, one sensual (Mitya), one clever (Ivan), and the youngest and best-beloved, who is most good (Alyosha). Much of the action moves in threes: besides the three brothers, there are three girls (Katerina, Lise, Grushenka), each of whom is courted by or attracted to, two Karamazov men; three chapters of confession that Mitya makes to Alyosha, and a further three made by Ivan to Alyosha; three ordeals Mitya suffers when arrested; three interviews between Ivan and the true murderer, his half-brother, the illegitimate Smerdyakov. Threes haunt the book, too, in the figure of 3000 rubles, the sum Katerina gives Mitya to mail to her, but which he partly squanders and then desperately tries to raise; the sum Karamazov keeps to bribe Grushenka to come to him; the extra sum he wishes to get from the peasant Lyagavy for a wood; the sum Mitya offers Grushenka's Polish seducer, to bribe him to leave her; the sum Mitya is thought to have stolen from his father when he murdered him. Even the Petersburg lawyer's fee for defending Mitya is 3000 rubles.

The first of the twelve constituent books gives us family history, and the second the preliminary scandal at the monastery where Alyosha attends the good and dying Zossima. The action, as usual, moves in concentrated bursts of time—from the scandal to the murder is four days; Mitya's trial and young Ilyusha's death in the last book constitute another compressed band of time.

THE SCENE OF SCANDAL

The novel is set in the town of Skotoprigonyevsk—meaning 'the beast-pen'—where Fyodor Pavlovich Karamazov has fathered a number of sons. He is a dissolute small landowner, an ill-natured and licentious clown, preposterous and muddleheaded in, we are told, the Russian style. He marries Adelaida Miusov, beautiful, wealthy and a girl of character, and cheats her out of her 25,000-ruble inheritance. She had eloped with him from caprice, and, following the marriage's failure, runs away with a graduate of a religious seminary, abandoning her three-year-old child, Mitya. Karamazov neglects the child, turning his home into a bawdy-house, holding orgies of drinking and general misbehaviour. Despite his debauchery and general neglect of Mitya, Dostoevsky takes care to warn us early on that, like all wrongdoers—'like we, ourselves'—he was more naïve and artless than we generally assume. Here Dostoevsky warns us against facile judgements: he seeks not merely our belief, as readers, but also our direct involvement.

Karamazov's second marriage is to the sixteen-year-old beauty Sophia Ivanovna, an orphan who has attempted suicide to evade her tormenting and tyrannical 'protectress'. His behaviour now deteriorates. He invites whores home for orgies while his wife is in the house. She understandably develops a nervous disease, and dies after eight years of maltreatment, leaving two sons, Ivan and Alyosha, to suffer a similar neglect to that already undergone by Mitya. All three are brought up by servants and distant relatives. At the point where the plot begins, the family meet up again, and more or less as complete strangers, whose discovery of one another forms a major strand in the story.

One further episode in Karamazov's life is chronicled. Coming home one evening in a company of 'gay young blades', he encounters a solitary half-wit, 'stinking Lizaveta' and, in response to a bet, rapes her, while the mourning-band for his first wife is still on his hat. Since the cook, Smerdyakov, who kills Karamazov, is the child of this perverse union, the novel has been read as one of moral come-uppance: his mother dies in childbirth, in wretchedness and misery, while the son later takes revenge for the father's multiple betrayals. But this grossly simplifies the tale, which scarcely advocates vengeance, and which does not emphasise this world as a place in which merit is necessarily rewarded or vice punished. No consoling victory in the perpetual battle between good and evil is promised, either in the individual heart or at large: only, at best, a renewal of the necessary struggle.

Mitya, the eldest, was taken in by the servant Grigory, then by his cousin Miusov, who early recounts Karamazov's seeming puzzlement that he even had a son. Miusov, too, then forgets about him and, after two further 'adoptions', a riotous army career complete with duel and demotion to the ranks, Mitya becomes involved in a lengthy struggle with his father over his inheritance from his wealthy mother. The father fobs off the son with occasional handouts, which the son regards as interest on his birthright, while the wilier father accounts them as discharging his debt.

The scandalous scene that opens the tale is set in the local monastery, where Alyosha is the favourite of the elder Zossima, the novel's dying saint and spokesman for the good life, in the truest sense. Karamazov has jokingly proposed this venue as an apt one for him and Mitya to make up their differences. What ensues is among the most painful and comical of Dostoevsky's scenes of scandal, containing a notable prophetic moment. Karamazov has by this stage degenerated both in appearance and in inner life, to an arrogant, bloated and inconsequential clown, with a long, cruel mouth, full lips and black, decaying stumps of teeth, and the general *mien* of a decadent Roman.

PARODY AND INNUENDO

Ivan, Karamazov and Miusov, a foolish, rich 1840s liberal with his inadequate 'culture', arrive first. Karamazov is full of sniggering innuendo. He has already been established for us as a man who plays his best respects to religion and the Ideal through blasphemous parody—when his first wife died he had shouted the opening of the *Nunc dimittis:* 'Lord, now lettest Thou Thy servant depart in peace'. He now develops a running joke about monasteries, with concubines and secret passages to 'the ladies'.

On arrival he mimics Miusov's 'society' bow to the monks, and this prepares us for the monkey-like role he plays throughout: the aping of the 'higher' by the 'lower' the negative but comic tribute paid by vice to virtue. Dostoevsky surely intends the comedy just as much as he intends us to see Karamazov's antics as perverse and destructive. In pretending homage to the good Zossima, 'Holy elder', 'your reverence', 'blessed man' and 'most holy being' are some of the terms he invents, undermining honour through excess, to both our acute embarrassment and our delight. He renews this strategy when he unexpectedly kneels and asks how he can gain eternal life, and when, in mock-religious language, he blesses the womb that bore Zossima and especially the 'tits' that 'gave thee suck'.

He tells pointless, banal puns, tests the elder through a

mock-artless question about a martyred saint purported to have kissed his own decapitated head, acts the saintly fool—the point about a *true* saintly fool being precisely that, unlike Karamazov, he would be unwitting. Karamazov's antics display his profound insincerity, and his lack of any real peace of conscience. 'A disgraceful comedy', Mitya exclaims when he belatedly arrives, and Karamazov explains, with an insolent humility, that he has staged this comedy of disgrace in order to test Zossima—after also proposing that he makes a fool of himself in order to be better liked. Neither explanation exhausts his complex motives, and Zossima, dealing with the situation with a patient good cheer despite the fact that he is ill and dying, advises him to cease lying.

A HARROWING CONTRAST

Zossima momentarily leaves the Karamazov contingent to attend to some patiently waiting peasant woman. One poor woman has lost all four of her children but cannot cease grieving for the last. This is an important, as well as a harrowing, scene, for both Ivan and Zossima are to preach on the death and suffering of children. 'If only I could see him', she exclaims, and is advised to allow time to heal her. A second awaits news of her son in Siberia and is told, accurately, that he is still alive. The scene introduces the themes of faith and of patient suffering. The suffering of children, in particular, stands in this novel as [the ultimate] of evil and of incomprehensible human pain.

Truth and Imagination in *The Brothers Karamazov*

Victor Terras

Whether in search of hard fact or spiritual revelation, the characters in *The Brothers Karamazov* spend much energy in pursuit of truth. Because Dostoyevsky ultimately comes down on the side of religion, one might imagine that the most moral of the characters in the novel would also be the most enlightened. This is not the case, however, as we see through the example of Ippolit Kirillovich. Though a good man, the prosecutor in Dmitry's case is blind to the fact that he is convicting the wrong person. And, inversely, a largely loathsome character like Father Karamazov uses his tremendous insight for the most unsavory of purposes. Critic Victor Terras explains how lack of imagination limits the vision of some characters to simple reason and how imagination offers others a wide vision of the world. Thus imagination rather than spirituality or moral fiber is what enlightens both the evil and the righteous in the novel.

Dostoevsky's preoccupation with "fact" and "details of fact" is well known. The power of the simple, concrete fact often becomes apparent in *The Brothers Karamazov*. Dmitry struggles with the facts of life (he calls them *realizm*) from beginning to end. But then, too, the figure of fiction appears just as prominently, and with the same power.

The first illustration of the power of a "mere" fiction appears as early as in the first chapter of Book I: a young woman, without any factual reason, commits suicide only because in her imagination she sees herself as [*Hamlet's*] Ophelia. Dostoevsky was fascinated by the power of fiction no less than by that of a "simple fact." A notebook entry sug-

From Victor Terras, "The Art of Fiction as a Theme in *The Brothers Karamazov*," in *Dostoevsky: New Perspectives*, edited by R.L. Jackson, ©1984. Adapted by permission of Prentice-Hall, Inc., Upper Saddle River, N.J.

gests that he was delighted to find an example of it in [the writings of Roman historian] Tacitus, where the story of one Vibulenus is told, who successfully incited his fellow soldiers to mutiny with an impassioned account of the cruel death of his brother—who later turned out to have been a mere figment of his imagination. And so it is the fiction of the open door as much as the fact of the brass pestle in the grass that convicts Dmitry.

An ironic *quid pro quo* of fact and fiction runs through the whole novel. An imaginary 3,000 rubles are as potent a factor in the plot as a real 3,000 rubles, or rather more so. In a display of ingenious as well as painstaking novelistic craftsmanship, Dostoevsky introduces a whole series of details which implant in the minds of several witnesses the erroneous notion that Dmitry was in possession of 3,000 rubles the night of his father's murder. One actually wonders if Dostoevsky is not polemicizing with [German philosopher] Immanuel Kant's famous disquisition on the difference between an imaginary 100 Thalers and 100 real Thalers.

TRUTH COMES AS INSPIRATION

All this raises the question of what connection—if any—there is between truth on the one hand and "fact" or "fiction" on the other. Insofar as Dostoevsky was convinced that art is an avenue to truth, and art is of course part fact and part fiction, this question becomes directly relevant to Dostoevsky's philosophy of art.

In the very introduction to the novel, the narrator asserts that a strange and somewhat eccentric, rather than a familiar, "average" character, may carry "within himself the very heart of the whole." Then very early on in the novel, the narrator develops a curious notion of what makes a man a "realist." It would seem that a realist is a person who lives and thinks in terms of an immediately or intuitively given reality. The opposite is, then, a "theoretician," who seeks to create and to realize a rational world of his own making. This makes Alyosha a "realist" and Rakitin a "theoretician."

Dmitry, after many trials and tribulations, comes to observe that, unlike in fiction, little accidents, not great events, destroy men in real life. He calls this "realism." Now, the contemporary theory of realism taught that the typical, rather than the fortuitous, should reign in fiction. Dostoevsky not only subscribed to this opinion but also believed that it was ultimately true of "real life" as well. So Dmitry is wrong when he sees himself as a victim of trivial accidents. He will realize this later in the novel. Similarly, the devil's suggestion that the truth is unhappily "almost always banal" . . . is another thesis advanced only to be refuted. Likewise, the notion that human life is a mere dream or illusion appears only as a warning to those of little faith: Mme. Khokhlakov is the case in point.

One thing is clear: those who pursue the truth rationally, confident of their human reason, are led into error. The truth will come to men through intuition or as inspiration. The distance from the truth of each character in the novel is measured by the power and quality of his—or her—imagination.

Stories, Teachings, and Predictions

Fyodor's perverse mind and amoral character would suggest that he is far from the truth. But with the exception of Smerdyakov, he intuitively understands everybody and everything very well. In fact, while he is blind to Smerdyakov's murderous intentions, he correctly recognizes the lackey's basic flaw: the man lacks imagination, his sharp intelligence being entirely practical. Dostoevsky actually seems to have aimed at endowing Fyodor with an almost uncanny clairvoyance. He asks Alyosha to leave the monastery only minutes after Father Zosima did. He speaks the mysterious and prophetic words, *"Da, Dmitriia Fedorovich eshche ne sushchestvuet."* As so often, his verbal clowning (here, "Dmitry Fyodorovich does not exist as yet" instead of "Dmitry Fyodorovich isn't here yet") leads to the utterance of a deep truth. Fyodor's assessment of Ivan's personality is correct, within the limits of Fyodor's own mind. He may be predicting his own fate when he projects the image of von Sohn, old lecher and victim of an obscene murder, on the "landowner" Maksimov, clearly a "double" of Fyodor's.

Dmitry, a man of the senses and, like his father, a raconteur and lover of beauty, though of a finer mold, is gifted with intuition, empathy, and imagination. He is never too far from the truth. His marvelous gift of language lets him utter the most profound truths in palpable poetic form. He also has a sense of humor and a keen ear for any sort of dissonance. Dmitry intuitively senses the sterility and ugliness of Rakitin's positivism. He senses it immediately when Alyosha falls into "Jesuit" casuistry, repeating in effect an argument of Smerdyakov's, in trying to save his brother.

Alyosha is the author of Father Zosima's *Vita.* Throughout the novel he also echoes his teacher's words and teachings. It is surely significant that, more than Dmitry, he is susceptible to the temptations of reason, visited upon him through his brother Ivan and his friend Rakitin. His teacher's shining example leads him back to the truth. Alyosha is a youth of delicate sensitivity and vivid imagination.

Ivan Karamazov, author of "The Grand Inquisitor," which he calls a "poem," also of an earlier poem "A Geological Cataclysm" and other works, is by far the most literate of the Karamazovs. His destruction as an author, which goes hand in hand with his downfall as a man, is one of Dostoevsky's main concerns in the novel. "The Grand Inquisitor" is undermined even from within through introduction of false notes, dissonances, melodrama, and inner contradictions, as well as by some telltale signs that the Grand Inquisitor is no prince of the Church or glamorous Miltonic Satan, but a "silly student, who never wrote two lines of poetry," as Ivan says himself. The "poem" is, of course, totally demolished later by its parody in the ninth chapter of Book XI. Nor is this development unprepared. Many earlier hints act as fuses that will eventually explode Ivan's edifice. When the Grand Inquisitor develops his concept of a group of "clever people" (*umnye liudi*) who rule mankind by giving it bread, mystery, and authority (in fact, though, an unkept promise, magic, and tyranny), one is reminded of Fyodor's cynical comments on "us clever people who'll sit snug, drinking their brandy." The chapter that concludes Book V is entitled "It's Always Worthwhile Speaking to a Clever Man." We know the definition of a "clever man" in all three instances: he is someone who has discovered that there is no God and uses his discovery to his advantage. Ivan, the "clever man," finds himself in the company of two other "clever people," Fyodor and Smerdyakov.

Like the Karamazovs, many characters of lesser importance are determined very largely by the products of their imagination: Grushenka by the fiction of her first love and by her tale of the onion, Katerina Ivanovna by her perverse dream of a life devoted to Dmitry, Liza by her fantasies, alternately sweet and cruel. Some characters we know virtually from their fictions only, such as Maksimov or Father Ferapont.

THE CONVICTION OF AN INNOCENT MAN

We know Dmitry's prosecutor, Ippolit Kirillovich, and his defender, Fetyukovich, almost exclusively through the products of their imagination. The former, a positivist and believer in psychology as an exact science, is an honest man and nobody's fool. But he has an ordinary imagination. He quickly creates a plausible account of the crime and an equally plausible image of the criminal. The prosecutor's version of what happened that fateful night is, however, based on two fictions: Grigory's honest mistake about the open door, which was really closed, and Smerdyakov's clever insinuations. The prosecutor also ignores a key fact that speaks in Dmitry's favor: the discrepancy between the amount of money found on Dmitry and the balance between 3,000 rubles and the money spent by Dmitry.

Ippolit Kirillovich exposes each statement made by the accused as a clumsy fiction, which he demolishes by the logic of his own version. In fact, though, everything Dmitry says is the truth, while the prosecutor's version is false. In particular, the prosecutor fails to see that the screw of psychological analysis can always be given another turn: Dmitry's fumbling and "giving himself away" may be evidence of his guilt, but it also may be evidence of his innocence: an innocent man might blunder and fall into a trap that a guilty man, who would be on his guard, would see. [In *Crime and Punishment,* for example,] Raskolnikov, who does not fall into Porfiry's trap, is a case in point. In fact, Dmitry's vivid imagination creates evidence against him, for instance, when he blurts out that the money was under his father's pillow—which he couldn't have known unless he was the murderer. Ippolit Kirillovich, a good man, simply underestimates the complexity of human nature. He is satisfied when he has proved Dmitry's story to be absurd, forgetting that the truth is sometimes absurd.

The narrator's condescending attitude toward Ippolit Kirillovich suggests that he is believed by the townspeople to be a nice enough, but somewhat limited person. Yet, against all expectations, he triumphs over the redoubtable Fetyukovich. He never suspects that he has convicted an innocent man, certainly the last thing he would have wanted. It is somewhat of a surprise that Ippolit Kirillovich expresses many of the ideas which we know were Dostoevsky's own, as is readily demonstrated by comparing his speech to passages in

Dostoevsky's *Diary of a Writer.* Dostoevsky, like Ippolit Kirillovich, was a believer in Holy Russia, "her principles, her family, everything she holds sacred." Ironically, these principles are upheld by the conviction of an innocent man.

The defender Fetyukovich is the exact opposite of Ippolit Kirillovich. He has his facts right. He can see through Smerdyakov. With perspicacity and intuition he reconstructs almost the entire course of events as they actually happened. He knows that he is skating on thin ice and skillfully slurs over the dubious steps in his argument. Fetyukovich says outright that the prosecutor's version of the events is open to the very same charge he had made against Dmitry's version, namely that it is a fiction: "What if you've been weaving a romance and about quite a different kind of man?" Fetyukovich reminds his opponent that one's image of another person is necessarily a fiction and that the real question is: how close is this fiction to the truth? He sarcastically calls the prosecutor's theory by which he had tried to prove premeditation on Dmitry's part "a whole edifice of psychology" and promptly demolishes it. He will not deny that his own version is a fiction, too. In fact, he will boldly admit that it is just that. But the fact of the matter is that Fetyukovich's version happens to be true.

Fetyukovich is called an "adulterer of thought." His shallow liberalism is clearly odious to the narrator (and to Dostoevsky). Moreover, there is reason to believe that he thinks Dmitry is really guilty. When he swears "by all that is sacred" that he believes in Dmitry's innocence, he is probably perjuring himself. And, last but not least, he loses his case, as the "jury of peasants" chooses to believe Ippolit Kirillovich.

In many ways the duel between Ippolit Kirillovich and Fetyukovich may be seen as an allegory of Dostoevsky's effort in *The Brothers Karamazov.* It was his swan song, much as Ippolit Kirillovich's oration was his. Like Fetyukovich, Dostoevsky pleads a difficult case in which the odds seem to be against the accused. The accused is God, the charge that He has created a world in which injustice and innocent suffering are allowed to prevail. Like Fetyukovich, Dostoevsky pleads his case with skill and eloquence, and is not above an occasional *argumentum ad hominem,* slurring over inconvenient details, and discrediting the witnesses for the prosecution. Especially the latter: Dostoevsky makes sure to destroy the reputation of every atheist in the novel.

IMAGINATION INDEPENDENT OF MORALITY

Could it be that Dostoevsky, like Fetyukovich, does not believe in the truth of his version of the case? This is really immaterial: Fetyukovich certainly does his best to save Dmitry. Nor is it his fault that the accused is found guilty. A conscientious and unbiased jury should have found Dmitry innocent. Similarly, Dostoevsky certainly wants God to win and does his best to ensure that He does. Still, Dostoevsky will lose his case with most readers. Like Fetyukovich's jury, they are biased, biased against God. Or, also like Fetyukovich's jury, they lack the imagination to follow Dostoevsky's intricate metaphysical argument.

In any case, Dostoevsky assigns the voice of truth to the man with the greater imagination, that is, to the artist (there is no question as to the great powers of Fetyukovich's imagination), and he does so regardless of the man's moral qualities. He also lets a jury of peasants reject the truth. The moral of the tale is then that an honest and well-meaning, but pedestrian man is prone to deep error and acts of grave injustice. It is Grigory, righteous and devout, but also an obtusely unimaginative man who gives the false evidence that convicts Dmitry. To attain the truth requires imagination, empathy, and inspiration.

Ippolit Kirillovich tries to put down Dmitry, saying: "To be sure, we are poets." The irony backfires, of course. Not only is Dmitry a poet, but he also knows more about the truth of life than the pedestrian prosecutor ever will. In the world of *The Brothers Karamazov*, everybody knows his or her measure of facts, and everybody must create his or her own fiction of the world. The poet's fiction is closest to the truth. The less a person is a poet, the farther removed is he or she from the truth. Significantly, it is Smerdyakov who advances the Russian nihilists' arguments against poetry, which Dostoevsky had combated all his life and which are thus denounced as a lackey's view of poetry. Rakitin's "polemic" with [Russian poet Aleksandr] Pushkin serves the same purpose. All and sundry nonpoets and antipoets in *The Brothers Karamazov* are hopelessly removed from the truth as Dostoevsky sees it, as well as from seeing the truth in the Karamazov murder case.

Father Karamazov as Buffoon

Jan van der Eng

In his deeply disturbing final novel, *The Brothers
Karamazov,* Dostoyevsky uses comic relief to foreshadow events, add complexity to difficult themes,
and break tension between characters. In the following passage, transcribed from a lecture at Stockholm
University, Dutch scholar Jan van der Eng selects
one scene of a particular meeting in the monastery
to illustrate how old Karamazov becomes a willing
clown in order to amuse himself and manipulate
others. Without the formalities one might expect
from a meeting in a holy place, Old Karamazov uses
everyday language or colloquialisms, in a kind of
calculated "innocence." This deliberate naïveté en-
ables him to pass off insults as ignorance and the
reader is able to see his true character. Because the
colloquialisms are exaggerated, we see his insinceri-
ties. While we are laughing, however, these insincer-
ities indicate major character flaws and serve to create tension even as they release it.

Comic relief often accompanies or follows upon scenes of
high tension, of fatal importance, of religious or philosophical significance. The comic effect originates from some kind
of incongruity between these scenes and the intervening or
following elements. A sort of clash occurs, which breaks the
tension and provokes laughter. The intervening elements,
moreover, often give ironic overtones to moments of religious or philosophical depth. Frequently the comic relief
does not only bring momentary lessening of the anxiety
caused by strained scenes, but also introduces new dramatic
complications. Comic relief appears mostly as a result of the
conversation between the characters. This is hardly surpris-

From Jan van der Eng, "A Note on Comic Relief in *The Brothers Karamazov,*" in *"The
Brothers Karamazov" by F.M. Dostoevskij,* by Jan van der Eng and Jan M. Meijer,
Dutch Studies in Russian Literature, vol. 2 (Paris: Mouton, 1971). Copyright ©1971
Mouton and Company N.V., Publishers, The Hague. Reprinted by permission of Mou-
ton de Gruyter, a division of Walter de Gruyter and Company.

ing, as several characters play definite comic and sometimes even clownish rôles: thus for instance the old clown Karamazov, the lady Chochlakova, Ivan's double the devil, the landowner Maksimov and still others. All of these figures deliberately make fools of themselves, except madame Chochlakova, who is quite innocent in her incoherent chatter. The incongruous themes, which make their way into the novel through a dialogue which at times almost passes into monologue, receive much of their comic flavour from the lexical and syntactical peculiarities that characterize the speech of certain figures.

The term 'comic relief' might be considered inadequate on the grounds that 'relief' does not at the same time indicate increasing complication and that 'comic' does not cover the humorous and the ironical element. It has been said by the philosopher Henri Bergson that comic elements are connected with outer effects of a person's defective adaptation to normal spontaneous processes of behaviour, thought, and so on. To laugh at a comic person is to deride his defective appearance without having any interest in his being.

Humour was defined by Dostoevskij himself as the sharp wit of deep concern. When humour appears, the *vis comica* [comic force] of deficient adaptation falls into the background. Adaptive deficiency then serves as a sign of some quality of a person and the smile it provokes includes acknowledgement of this quality. This will be still more so when a person uses irony, that is to say, figures of speech in which the deficiency is expressed in words apparently indicating the opposite. If we persist in using the formula 'comic relief', it is not to deny the humorous and ironic shades, nor the intensification of tragic conflicts as a result of what at first glance might seem mere comicalness—we use this formula to stress the fact that in Dostoevskij's novel some sort of clash between two systems of behaviour, thought and so on, precedes the humour, the irony and the tragic complication, and that relief, in the sense of momentary ease from the tension in strained situations, developments or arguments, is the primary effect.

A SHARP WIT

As I have said already, comic incongruities mostly appear as a consequence of the conversation of more or less clownish characters. The most outstanding buffoon is of course old

Karamazov. His buffoonery becomes particularly expressive in the scenes laid in the monastery. It is sharp-witted buffoonery, as the old man is not only enjoying the clash between on the one side the vile, erotic and pestering element he introduces into the cell in his own person, and on the other side the devout monastic atmosphere: he tries at the same time to show up what he considers the emptiness of religious practices, of the monastic way of life; he insinuates that the devout appearance hides either naïveté or, more probably, a way of life not so very different from his own.

Thus there is in the first place comic incongruity, the clash between the burlesque element and the monastic element; and secondly there is irony brought about by his allusions to the coexistence of discordant qualities: religious and moral superiority are in his opinion either built on naïveté or else erected as a camouflage for normal aspirations to earthly well-being. One might say that the insinuations of an opposition between solemn pretensions and human conditions give a witty and deepening perspective to Karamazov's burlesque behaviour in monastic surroundings. The purely comical element has thus been surpassed. Concern has been aroused for his wit, for his person. There is a spark of tragic humour. Relief means here the momentary postponement of the financial conflicts which had reached a burning point.

Old Karamazov plays several rôles to bring about a comical clash and to express at the same time his ironical insinuations. He assumes the rôle of the submissive believer performing ritual acts, the rôle of the worldly man amazed at the monastic way of life, the rôle of the faithful believer, shocked by the abuses in a centre of christian living, the rôle of the indignant believer criticizing the decay of the christian ideas in the monastic sphere, the rôle of the worldly man challenging the monks that there is more true christian spirit in what they consider a depraved way of life than in their monastic cult. Often these rôles fuse in the course of his buffooning provocation. And always, of course, they take on a bizarre appearance in contrast to the indecent, disgusting person the father is.

HUMOR WITH A PURPOSE

At the beginning of the novel the old Karamazov decided upon a meeting in the elder Zosima's cell under the pretext of coming to an agreement with his eldest son about the inheritance. The financial conflict, however, remains for the moment in the background: Dmitrij, the eldest son, will, as we know, arrive much too late. Meantime the old father performs a sort of 'one-man-show'. Approaching the gates of the hermitage, he at once assumes the rôle of the submissive believer: he suggests by his words and acts that entering into this rôle is like getting into another coat. He says: "when in Rome do as the Romans", crossing himself fervently before the images of the saints painted above and on the sides of the gates. The next moment old Karamazov insinuates the emptiness of the monastic ideal by mentioning in the same breath incongruous elements of the monastic way of life:— "There are altogether", he observes, "twenty-five saints seeking salvation in this hermitage, looking at one another and eating cabbage soup". Then he plays himself in the rôle of the baffled worldly man full of amazement at such a life and hinting obliquely at more normal human practices behind the devout appearance— "What is so remarkable", he says, "is that no woman is allowed to enter these gates. And that is quite true, you know. But, he suddenly addressed a monk, I've heard that the elder receives ladies. He does, doesn't he?" At the answer of the monk that there are two little rooms for ladies outside the hermitage wall, old Karamazov tortuously emphasizes his insinuation, seemingly withdrawing his previous words. At the same time he affects belief in the monastic rule: by this affectation he manages to lay bare what he considers the absurdity of the rule: —"Oh, so there is a secret passage from the hermitage to the ladies! Please, holy father, don't think I am suggesting anything. I'm just making a statement of fact. You know, on Mount Athos– you've heard of it, haven't you?—not only women but any creatures of the female sex are not allowed—no hens, no turkey-hens, no calves. . . ." Again and again the old man adds force to the incongruous element he introduces into the cell in his own person: now he compares himself with a king, then with the [French] philosopher [Denis] Diderot. He does so professing that he has had his doubts just like Diderot but is now sitting and waiting for words of great wisdom. The next moment, however, he quotes words out of context and in connection with this ironical overtones are given to life based on such formulas. This comes to the fore in the following anecdote:—"I'm just like the philosopher Diderot, your reverence. I suppose, most holy father, that the philosopher Diderot went to see the Metropolitan Platon at the time of the Empress Catherine. As soon as he went in, he blurted out: 'There is no God'. To which his holiness, the great patriarch, raised his finger and said: 'The madman hath said in his heart there is no God'. And the philosopher threw himself down at his feet at once: 'I believe,' he cried, 'and I will be baptized'. So they baptized him there and then. Princess Dashkov was his godmother and Potyomkin his godfather." This anecdote of Diderot's baptism on the spot serves to hold up to ridicule the christian way of life, sponsored by such representatives of society-glamour and false appearances as for instance [Grigori] Potemkin. An ironic and hence negative colouring spreads from the hyperbolic addresses like "the great patriarch" into the words addressed to Zosima: "most holy father".

Father Karamazov challenges the monk's idea of a true christian spirit when they stigmatize as 'shame' his delighted gossip about Grušen'ka. "Why shame?"—he cries out—"This 'creature', this 'disreputable woman', gentlemen, is perhaps holier than all of you who are seeking salvation in this monastery.... She loved much, and Christ himself forgave the woman who loved much". At the interruption of father Joseph "Christ did not forgive for that kind of love" the old man replies: "Yes, for that kind of love, monks, for that very same kind of love. You're seeking salvation here by eating cabbage soup and you think you're righteous men! You eat gudgeons, a gudgeon a day, and you think you can buy God with gudgeons!"

AFFECTION, EXAGGERATION, AND VULGARITY

Old Karamazov's gossip introduced into the novel some scandalous details about Mitja's love affairs (Dmitrij, of course, had arrived at that moment). This piece of a 'chronique scandaleuse' is exploited by him to create another clash with the pious atmosphere and to denounce monastic formalism again. But the comic elements also function here as factors of conflict. As a matter of fact a new conflictive issue, which will determine to a large extent the further developments, finds its first oblique expression here: the rivalry between old Karamazov and his eldest son in courting Grušen'ka (This will be made more evident after some pages in the conversation between Rakitin and Aleša). The tension is, of course, increased by the fact that one of the antagonists vilipended [disparaged] the other's amorous passion while he passed over his own scandalous rôle. The reader, however, is not yet informed of the father's part, and he will surely take Dmitrij's words: 'can he be allowed to defile the earth by his existence' and the reply: "listen to the parricide" as comical hyperboles. But the reader will perhaps remember them afterwards, as they are echoed and paraphrased in the words of quite a range of characters. The conflictive centre of the comic elements explodes like a delayed bomb-shell. It may be said that all the scenes in the cell which turn around the father's performance will heighten the atmosphere of conflict. This may be not only true in connection with Dmitrij. The second son Ivan also could accumulate in such scenes the sensations of disgust and hatred that later on will provoke his bitter words: "one reptile devours another!" Ivan is the only son present at the last scene in the monastery. Old Karamazov plays then the rôle of the faithful believer shocked by the decay of monastic asceticism and discipline. He affects to be upset by the old port wine and the medoc he sees on the table in the Father's Superior's dining-room: "Well, well, Fathers! That doesn't look like gudgeons" [a kind of fish, but also, as a pun, people who are duped]. In his indignant reactions clichés from the progressive press are used: "And who has supplied you with it all? The toiling Russian peasant bringing you the farthings earned by his horny hands wresting them from his family. . . . Why, Holy Fathers, you suck the blood of the people!" In the end he enters almost into a paroxysm of simulated feeling denouncing the monks' lust for money and their heresy-hunting, of which he proclaims himself a scandalized victim. And again the progressive clichés appear: "This monastery has meant a lot in my life. I have shed bitter tears for it! You used to set my wife, the shrieker, against me. You cursed me with bell, book and candle. You spread stories about me all over the district. Enough, Fathers, this is the age of liberalism, the age of steamers and railways. Not a thousand, not a hundred roubles, not a hundred kopecks will you get out of me."

After a biblical quotation pronounced by the Father Superior, which is meant to exorcize the evil spirits that haunt the old man, he bursts out: "Tut-tut-tut! Sanctimonious old phrases! Old phrases and old gestures! Old lies and conventional obeisances!" and so on. Even these translated fragments will show that a great deal of the comic, humorous and ironical effect is in the successfully created illusion of vivid colloquial usage in addition to a particular touch of lexical, syntactical and intonational means. There are effective intonational suggestions, brought about by the old rhetorical devices, such as elliptic questions and exclamations. Fixed colloquialisms with a well-known tone pattern are used to suggest the moments of affected amazement, indignation and so on. Parallelism of syntactical units underlines increasingly emotional utterances. The meddling of vulgarisms, archaisms and barbarisms creates along with the impression of vividness a tinge of comic incoherence. So does the range of incoherent semantic units gathered up in one syntactical link. A special comic effect arises from the infiltration in his speech of progressive notes strongly clashing with notes of a more solemn character.

CHRONOLOGY

1821

Fyodor Mikhaylovich Dostoyevsky is born November 11 in Moscow

1825

Death of Czar Alexander; coronation of Nicholas I

1837

Death of mother, Mariya; death of poet Aleksandr Pushkin; Fyodor and Mikhail leave for engineering school

1839

Father's murder

1843

Dostoyevsky graduates from military engineering academy, begins work in St. Petersburg

1844

Quits his government job

1846

Poor Folk is published; begins attending the Petrashevsky meetings

1849

Arrested and sentenced to Siberia

1854

Posted to the military battalion in Semipalatinsk for the balance of his sentence; Crimean War begins

1855

Death of Nicholas I; Dostoyevsky becomes a low-ranking officer

1856

Promoted to second lieutenant

1857

Marries Mariya Dmitriyevna Isayeva; *A Little Hero* is published

1858

Dostoyevsky and Mariya leave Semipalatinsk for Tver

1859

Returns to St. Petersburg

1860

Brother, Mikhail, receives permission to publish *Time; Memoirs from the House of the Dead* is published

1861

The Insulted and Injured is published

1862

First trip to western Europe

1863

Time shut down by censors; Dostoyevsky meets Appolinariya Suslovna in Paris on his second trip to western Europe; *Winter Notes on Summer Impressions* is published

1864

The first issue of *Epoch* appears; Mariya dies; Mikhail dies; *Notes from the Underground* is published

1865

Travels in western Europe

1866

Crime and Punishment appears in the *Russian Messenger;* Anna Grigorevna Snitkina transcribes *The Gambler*

1867

Marriage to Anna; Dostoyevsky and his new wife go abroad and live in several western European cities

1868

Daughter Sonya is born and dies in Geneva, Switzerland

1869

Daughter Lyubov is born in Dresden, Germany

1872

Return to St. Petersburg; son Fyodor is born; *The Possessed* is published

1873

Becomes editor of the *Citizen*

1875

Son Alyosha is born

1876

Begins publishing monthly journal *Diary of a Writer*

1877

Spends two days with his sister in their old home at Daravoye

1878

Alyosha dies; Dostoyevsky visits the monastery Optina Pustyn to see Father Ambrose, the holy monk

1879

The Brothers Karamazov is published

1880

Delivers famous "Pushkin Speech" at dedication of Pushkin monument

1881

Dostoyevsky dies February 9

FOR FURTHER RESEARCH

Harold Bloom, ed., *Modern Critical Views: Fyodor Dostoevsky.* New York: Chelsea House, 1989.

Joseph Frank and David I. Goldstein, eds., *The Selected Letters of Dostoyevsky.* New Brunswick, NJ: Rutgers University Press, 1987.

Ronald Hingley, *The Undiscovered Dostoyevsky.* Westport, CT: Greenwood Press, 1962.

Stanislaw Mackiewicz, *Dostoyevsky.* London: Munro Press, 1947.

Robin Feuer Miller, *The Brothers Karamazov: Worlds of the Novel.* New York: Twayne, 1992.

Konstantin Mochulsky, *Dostoevsky: His Life and Work.* Princeton, NJ: Princeton University Press, 1967.

Robert Payne, *Dostoyevsky: A Human Portrait.* New York: Knopf, 1967.

Richard Peace, *Dostoyevsky: An Examination of the Major Novels.* Cambridge, England: Cambridge University Press, 1971.

Ivan Roe, *The Breath of Corruption: An Interpretation of Dostoievsky.* Port Washington, NY: Kennikat Press, 1946.

Miriam T. Sajkovic, *F.M. Dostoevsky: His Image of Man.* Philadelphia: University of Philadelphia Press, 1962.

Ernest J. Simmons, *Dostoevsky: The Making of a Novelist.* New York: Vintage Books, 1940.

Edward Wasiolek, *Crime and Punishment and the Critics.* Belmont, CA: Wadsworth, 1961.

———, *Dostoevsky: The Major Fiction.* Cambridge, MA: MIT Press, 1964.

Rene Wellek, *Dostoevsky: A Collection of Critical Essays.* Englewood Cliffs, NJ: Prentice-Hall, 1962.

Avrahm Yarmolinsky, *Dostoevsky: Works and Days.* New York: Funk and Wagnalls, 1971.

L.A. Zander, *Dostoevsky.* Trans. Natalie Duddington. London: SCM Press, 1948.

WORKS BY FYODOR DOSTOYEVSKY

Poor Folk (1846)

The Double (1846)

Mister Prokharchin (1846)

The Landlady (1847)

A Novel in Nine Letters (1847)

An Honest Thief (1848)

White Nights (1848)

A Weak Heart (1848)

The Jealous Husband (1848)

A Christmas Tree and a Wedding (1848)

A Little Hero (1857)

A Friend of the Family (1859)

Uncle's Dream (1859)

The Village of Stepanchikovo and Its Inhabitants (1859)

Memoirs from the House of the Dead (1860)

The Insulted and Injured (1861)

Winter Notes on Summer Impressions (1863)

Notes from the Underground (1864)

Crime and Punishment (1866)

The Gambler (1867)

The Idiot (1868)

The Eternal Husband (1870)

The Possessed (1872) (also known as *The Devils*)

A Raw Youth (1875)

The Diary of a Writer (1876–1878)

The Brothers Karamazov (1879)

INDEX